THE RED

ROSE CREW

THE RED

ROSE CREW

*A True Story of Women,
Winning, and the Water*

D ANIEL   J .   B OYNE

With a New Foreword by David Halberstam

THE LYONS PRESS
Guilford, Connecticut
An imprint of the Globe Pequot Press

Copyright 2000, Daniel J. Boyne

First Lyons Press paperback edition, 2005

The Lyons Press is an imprint of The Globe Pequot Press.

10 9 8 7 6 5 4 3 2 1

Printed in the United States of America

Jacket photo: "Carie Graves, on the Power," © Arthur Grace

Designed by Abby Kagan

ISBN 1-59228-758-1

The Library of Congress has previously cataloged an earlier edition as follows:

Boyne, Daniel J.
The Red Rose Crew: a true story of women, winning, and the water /
Daniel J. Boyne.—1st ed.
       p.   cm
ISBN 0-7868-6622-5
1. Red Rose Crew (Rowing team) 2. Women rowers—
United States—Bibliography. I. Title
GV793.B69   2000
797.1'4'092273-dc21
[B]   00-031949

To my daughter, Mikaela

Acknowledgments

With thanks to the women of the Red Rose Crew and their coach, Harry Parker; Steve Gladstone, Jay Mimier, Sue Ela, Maggie MacLean, and Robert Graves; Alicia Gurney and the research staff at the Henley River and Rowing Museum; *The Henley Gazette*, Pat and Valerie at the Wheatsheaf Pub, Derek Thurgood, and Angus Robertson; Anita DeFrantz and The Women's Sports Foundation, Nigel Gallaher, Allen Rosenberg, Chris Baillieu, and Bernie Horton; the late Thomas Mendenhall, for his invaluable historical work in rowing, and Thomas Weil, Jr., for his current research; *Sports Illustrated* and Arthur Grace, for their excellent photos and insights; Karen Mittlestadt at USRowing; my wife, Karen Barss, for all of her help editing; and Lane Zachary, Jennifer Lang, and Larry Ashmead for their encouragement with the book.

F o r e w o r d

It is the spring of 1997. I am standing there at Lake Quinsigamond in western Massachusetts where the various high-school and prep-school crews are rowing in the regatta that is the culmination of half a year's work and training. My daughter is rowing in her school four. She is in the school's B boat. I have seen her row at earlier races and am impressed. She and the other three members of the boat are smooth if not powerful, and when I watch them I am caught again in the beauty of the sport, a beauty that reflects hours and hours of commitment. I am aware, as is she, that she will never be a great oar, and that she will not row in college, for she is slight, irate with her parents from her early childhood because she got neither her mother's nor her father's height. But she decided to row nonetheless and this year, rowing (something my wife and I will gradually come to understand), has become a manifestation of her dedication to her colleagues, and her willpower. For this brief stretch in her life rowing has become a reflection of who she is, and who she is going to be—intense, responsible, committed to those around her, purposeful and fearless.

Her crew is undefeated so far. If my memory serves correctly, there are five boats in the race. Hers has won an earlier trial, I believe. But in the final they get off to a terrible start. They are dead last after about 150 yards. And then they begin to feel their rhythm and there is a certain magical swing to their oars; the boat smoothes out, and they start passing the other boats. First one and then a second. My eye is fixed on her boat like a laser beam—four young women, perhaps seventeen years old—reaching as deeply as they can into themselves. There are still two boats ahead of theirs. On the shore my own heart feels like it is going to burst. I have rowed myself at a relatively low level, in eights and singles, nothing as intense as this with as much at stake, but I know the demands of this moment and the inevitability of the pain, and the fact that for these few minutes this is the only thing in the world that matters. They pass a third boat, and now they are closing on the lead boat, with probably 100 yards left. They close a little more—it is very tight at the end, but the other boat holds its position. They come in second.

My wife and I rush down to the dock to greet them. Our pride is beyond measurement. They are, of course, heartbroken: all they can think is that it is their first loss, and it was so close, and they were driving on the lead boat at the end. Another 100 yards and they might have won . . . perhaps. They are caught in the sheer misery of the moment, so much at stake, coming so close, missing by so little. My wife and I—older and perhaps wiser, with enough comparable defeats in our own lives when we were younger that magically someday morph into triumphs of character—are if not exhilarated, thrilled on their behalf by their courage, their comeback from that dreadful start, and what they accomplished against terrible odds. They think it is a defeat; we think it is a victory of great proportions, a reflection of something marvelous discovered within. I am apt to think of that day as a kind of epiphany: we will see more evidence of this in years to come—when she ends up teaching kindergarten in a poor area of the Deep South and stands up again and again to some of the darker forces in our society manifested in their crudest incarnations—but as I write this, I am reminded now that this is the first evidence of the power and strength of her spirit, and her willingness, when summoned, to find and give more of herself than anyone expected.

I thought of all this—what women's sports helped find and give to our daughter—as I read Daniel Boyne's *The Red Rose Crew*, about an American women's crew that came from nowhere to take second against all odds in an international race in 1975 in England, losing out to an East German crew by a few feet (with an awareness that the East German crew was, like nearly all athletic representatives of that dreadful country, almost surely coked to the gills with steroids). Boyne's is not only a very good book—actually quite a marvelous one—but it is a very important book as well. It's by far the best book that I know of the pioneer years when, against unspeakable odds and in the face of unpardonable stupidity and sexism, women's sports in America began to come of age. *The Red Rose Crew* is in fact a classic and it belongs on any number of lists: a list of sports thrillers (it's a great read, almost impossible to put down); a list of the changes wrought by the women's movement that began in the sixties; and finally a list of good books on American history—for it is a book that tells how things really happened and describes the formidable forces aligned against the women who led the way.

The young women in this book are pioneers—they triumphed not merely over the favored Russian and Romanian women in England, but also back in their own country against all the prejudices of the era about what women were not supposed to do. They triumphed despite poor, indeed unspeakable practice facilities; obtuse, disingenuous college athletic directors and ignorant rowing officials; and narrow-minded, smug male rowers (the gold for truly appalling behavior goes to the crude Yale oarsmen of that era). What they did was remarkable, standing up for themselves and for those yet unborn: one has a sense reading Boyne, that they were always aware of their dual responsibilities. They wanted to row for their own pleasure and rewards and felt they had earned the right to do so, but they were also acting for those still to come—their daughters, so to speak—asking the age old questions of those who challenge an outmoded, rotted hierarchy: If not us, who? and If not now, when?

Sometimes now when I lecture at a college someone will ask where all the heroes have gone—why don't we have heroes like Ted Williams or Joe DiMaggio, or other good athletes of their childhood? It is a fascinating question and it presupposes that there were heroes back then, and that someone who is a better baseball player because he had slightly better eyesight than his peers is indeed a hero. I have my own quirky list of heroes, and it rarely jibes with the conventional list accepted by those who decide these things. My heroes tend to have done something that matters in the long run, that changes things and makes this a more just and democratic society, and who in the process have often gone against the prevailing prejudices of the era. By that scale this is both a book and a boat filled with heroes. The millions of women like my daughter who have participated in different sports since the Red Rose Crew challenged the rules are in their debt. And I too, still the proud father from Lake Quinsig, remain in their debt.

There is one other hero in this book and he is an unlikely one. Boyne's book is in a way, whether intended or not, an homage to Harry Parker, the Harvard rowing coach. As I write this, Parker has been the varsity rowing coach there for forty-three years. It is arguable that he is not merely the dominating figure of American rowing over a stunningly long period, but that he may be the most successful, longest reigning coach operating at such a high level in American collegiate athletics. He is in all ways an admirable man, intelligent, careful, and talented; he is a stoic man himself and he has almost involuntarily taught, among other things, stoicism to the not-so-stoic children of a privileged part of our society. Several generations of oarsmen and now oarswomen (if a generation is fifteen years, we are talking about three generations) are better, stronger people because they had the good fortune to enter his world.

Parker is also the fairest of men, the most innately egalitarian. He was at the very top of his profession in 1975 when the young women in this book came to him asking for his help. Not surprisingly, if you know him, Parker, took up their challenge, and he did not let the prejudices of the era blind him as it did so many others in the world of intercollegiate athletics. He based his treatment of the women's crew as he would any other group of rowers—on their dedication and their talent. Thus the women Parker coached were neither the first nor the last to understand that he represents American amateur athletics at its very best: he took on their quest, as he has done so much else in his life, simply because it was the right thing to do.

So this is an uncommon book about an uncommon group of women—heroes for this or any other time.

David Halberstam
2005

"When one rows it is not the rowing which moves the ship: rowing is only a magical ceremony by means of which one compels a demon to move the ship."
——*NIETZSCHE*

"What is there in the universe more fascinating than running water and the possibility of moving over it? What better image of existence and possible triumph."
——*SANTAYANA*

FIRST
STROKES

O n e

A T THE 1956 NATIONAL ROWING CHAMPIONSHIPS
in Syracuse, New York, a three-year-old girl sat impa-
tiently beside her mother, waiting for her dad to row by. It
was difficult to wait, and it was difficult to be small. When a
woman sitting next to them in the bleachers suddenly dropped her
glasses, Carie got a lucky break. She was the only one small enough
to fit through the space in the seats where the glasses had disappeared. Momentarily, she felt very important. She was already
proud of the fact that she'd been chosen by her parents to attend
the regatta, while her younger brother and sister had been left
back in Spring Green, Wisconsin. Carie had lorded this over the
two of them, especially her brother, Ross, parading by him to the
car as he played in the sandbox at the baby-sitter's house.

Crew races were difficult events to watch, regardless of age or
experience. From the bleachers, located near the finish line, you
couldn't see the first half of the race or witness the crews going off
the starting line in a brilliant flurry of bodies and oars. If you had
really good eyes, or a decent set of binoculars, you might be able to
spot them from a distance of one mile—not the boats themselves

or even the people in them, but the regular, rhythmic flashing of the blades, feathering out of the water between strokes. This was one good reason to paint your oars a bright color, like the red blades of the Wisconsin crew slowly approaching the stands.

Early on in the history of the sport, various efforts had been made to help bring spectators within viewing distance of the crews. Railroads were built alongside rivers, like the Hudson in Poughkeepsie, where the Nationals had once been held. They were expensive to maintain, unreliable in speed, and still didn't put the audience close enough to the action. Spectator boats, which trailed behind the crews, had also been tried with mixed results. Some were decked out with jazz bands and served champagne, to give the event a more festive air. But here the problem was how to get close enough to the race without disturbing the crews, either with an errant wake or a noisy blast from the band.

In the end, these attempts hardly seemed worth the effort. Baseball, basketball, and football came along and attracted thousands of fans, all corralled in a central place. And while stadiums made money, rivers didn't. Beyond the logistics of watching a crew race, it was difficult to put a fence around a body of water that might stretch for miles in either direction. It was done in England, at Henley, but that was different. There, rowing had become an elitist sport, and Henley part of the British high social calendar.

American rowing had much more working-class roots. Some of the greatest American rowers were the sons of Irish immigrants hoping to better their social and financial status. Once the sport began to lose its support from the general public, it could not put on aristocratic airs. Consequently, it was reduced to a much lesser role and witnessed by a small audience of true aficionados. There were other reasons, too, why the fans drifted away: the lack of violence, or even contact, between the teams, the repetitive motion within a crew. Everyone seemed to do the same thing, and this lack of independent action among the players discounted the notion of individual stars. For all its teamwork ethic, America loved heroes.

Robert Graves, the captain of the Wisconsin varsity crew, was a hero in his own right. A Korean War veteran, he had been part of the first Army Raider unit, trained by British Commandos, and had earned a Silver Star for bravery. He was a man of great physical and moral stature. At 6 feet 5 inches and 205 pounds, he was big, even for an oarsman, and being older and more worldly-wise than most of the other men in the boat, he had an unspoken, commanding presence. When the rest of the team had tried to give him a regulation "crew cut" that spring, he had physically resisted several attempts with the razor, and a few of the perpetrators had gotten cut. Finally coach Norm Sanjou had suggested to the team that it might be better to just leave him alone.

The Wisconsin oarsmen were often quite large, and there were perennial jokes about the "farm boy" midwesterners. Bigger didn't always mean better, but the Badgers usually did well at the Nationals, generally placing in the top four of the six-boat final. Still, it was difficult for them to beat the Ivy League crews like Yale, who definitely upstaged them off the water, by coming to dinner dressed in their smart blue blazers.

To go along with their bright red blades, the Wisco crew had red shirts with a broad white band running straight down from each shoulder. As the crews came into view, Carie saw the blades first and then the bodies. Finally, she saw the boats themselves, just slivers of wood that were actually over sixty feet long, beautifully hand-crafted from mahogany or western red cedar. The shells were so narrow and rode so low in the water that on a choppy day at Lake Onandaga, a few waves could completely obscure them from view or even swamp the boat entirely. From a distance, especially in the eyes of a child, it looked like the people in the boats were somehow riding miraculously on top of the waves, with nothing underneath them.

The crews glided by the grandstand in a stately procession of oars, boats, and bodies. It was hard enough for Carie to make out the Wisconsin crew, let alone pick out her father in the five seat. Even for her mother, Dyrele, it was difficult to distinguish all the crews from one another and impossible to tell how hard the oarsmen were actually working. What they saw instead was a graceful, synchronous movement of bodies and oars that was almost mesmerizing. Had it not been for the shouting of the coxswains who steered the boats and called for more power, the whole thing might have seemed like a staged parade.

The close order of finish sustained the illusion. All five boats covered the 2000-meter course within seven seconds of one another. By crew standards, that was fairly tight racing. It meant that all the teams were worthy of one another, with barely a boat length separating first from last place.

Just the week before, on the very same lake, Wisconsin had finished third at the Intercollegiate Rowing Association Championships, competing against some of the same colleges. Over a grueling, three-mile course, they had even beaten their arch-rival, the University of Washington. Cornell and Navy had been first and second, respectively. It had been a decent day for the Badgers, who had edged out Stanford and UPenn—not to mention Princeton, Syracuse, and MIT. It always felt good to beat the East Coast teams, who had an air of superiority. So what if Harvard and Yale hadn't been there, engaged in their annual duel on the Thames, in New London, Connecticut—theirs was a snooty, private race that had been the very reason why the IRAs were created in 1895.

But for this race Yale *was* present, vying for the right to represent the U.S. at the Olympics. They crossed the finish line three seconds ahead of the pack, trailed closely by Cornell, Navy, and Washington. This time around, the Badgers finished last. It was Robert Graves' senior year, and not the best way to end his college rowing days.

But Wisconsin would be back to try again.

THE GRAVES FAMILY drove back to Madison together in their station wagon, while the rest of the team rode on the bus. A few years later, when Robert finished his graduate degree in landscape architecture, they packed up their Ford again and moved back to where he was born, just outside of Spring Green. Wyoming Valley, Wisconsin, was a small farming community with a population of 1200. The locals in nearby Spring Green sometimes referred to it as the "Valley of the God Almighty Joneses"—a begrudging tribute to the Welsh founding fathers, who happened to be the five uncles of Frank Lloyd Wright. Wright himself had extended his family's ownership of Wyoming Valley by developing a world famous fellowship of architects, known as Taliesin, right in the middle of the rural Wisconsin farmland.

It was an odd, oil-and-water mix—the conservative farmers and the bohemian members of the fellowship. Unsurprisingly, the two groups were often at odds with one another, especially during WWII and the Korean War, when the Taliesin group became conscientious objectors and were eventually looked upon by the locals as Communist sympathizers. The local business people refused to wait on them in various stores and restaurants, and even Carie's father, Robert, had a difficult time with this when he was growing up. It was only later that he managed to live in peace with both groups without being ostracized by either.

Robert's father established the original connection to Taliesin. He single-handedly managed the odd collection of farms, outbuildings, and architects' houses that lay within the 400-acre property. As a boy, Robert helped his dad with this work and inherited a fruitful tie to the Taliesin Fellowship, but it was one that sometimes made his friends suspicious. This distrust, and the treatment he received from merchants, may have influenced his decision to enlist in the Army and serve in the Korean War. He came back four years later with a Silver Star for bravery in action, leaving little doubt in anyone's mind as to his sense of patriotism.

He got married soon after, started having kids, and went back to school at the University of Wisconsin to finish his degree in landscape architecture. Taliesin had left its mark. So had the war. He was a man who did what he pleased and didn't care what others thought. The people of Spring Green, however, now treated him with such deference and respect that many began to refer to their town as the "Valley of the God Almighty Graveses."

His first daughter, Carie, was to inherit some of this strong sense of independence, as well as his looming physical presence. At 5 feet 10 inches, her mother wasn't small either, but Carie had her father's bones and inner temperament. By sophomore year in high school, she had already reached her full height of 6 feet 1 inch. It made her uncomfortable to be so tall. As she grew up, she also found it wasn't easy to live under the shadow of such a great man. Robert Graves was a stern disciplinarian, who had definite ideas about how his children should be raised.

Through his Taliesin connections, Graves leased and then bought a small farm, known as Aldebaren. While he went about his career as a landscape architect, his five children worked on the 160-acre property. They went to school with other farm kids in a tiny, two-room schoolhouse. It was a lifestyle that exposed them to the principle of hard work, but it was tempered by the bohemian atmosphere of Taliesin, with its constant influx of artists, writers, and actors from all over the world who were drawn to the rural community during the summer. These sophisticates brought with them an exotic approach to life that Carie had never seen before.

Even before she finished high school, Carie had begun to grow restless on the family farm and impatient with the restrictions imposed by her parents. At age sixteen, she spent a summer on a kibbutz in Israel as part of the Experiment in International Living, and learned a little more about life through the acquaintance of some city girls from New York and New Jersey. She came home smoking cigarettes, hemmed up her dress twice, and carried on with an attitude of carefree independence. When her parents informed her that she couldn't smoke on the premises, she simply walked down to the highway that defined the eastern boundary of their property and puffed away, standing on the edge of the asphalt. She threw her butts right into their mailbox, to make doubly sure they knew exactly what she was doing.

Her parents were mortified and totally unprepared for the rebellious behavior of their eldest child. By the time she graduated from high school, Carie had become insufferable and the tension between her and her parents had greatly escalated. Her mother resorted to small punishments to try to control her. But one day when Dyrele lost her temper and slapped her face, Carie simply turned her head the other way and said, "Would you like to slap the other cheek?" It was no use, and her mother knew it. Her daughter had become too much for her to handle, and any physical and mental advantage she held over her child had completely disappeared.

Carie was big, strong-willed, and knew that real life existed elsewhere, outside the perimeter of the 160-acre farm. Even her father had exhausted his influence. One day, toward the end of the summer, he instructed her to make everyone's sandwiches for lunch. She was the eldest child and this was one of her responsibilities. When Carie started throwing dishes around in protest, he suddenly flew into a fit of rage and ordered her to get out of the house. That was it, she decided. She knew her dad really didn't want her to leave for good, but she was stubborn and felt like she had to make a stand. So instead of returning home, she moved in with a friend and made plans to attend the University of Wisconsin. It was a short, forty-mile drive from Spring Green, and many of her high school friends were already enrolled there.

Madison was a lively college town that had more than its share of bars and breweries. If Wisconsin was a beer-brewing state, then Madison was one of the prime places to drink it. It was 1971 and a good year to be a young woman starting off on her own. Carie took advantage of all the social venues around campus, but she was also looking forward to the academic challenges of the university itself. By all outward appearances she was decidedly bohemian, with long chestnut hair parted down the middle and unshaven legs often covered by a pair of bell-bottoms. Underneath all this, however, lay a brooding mind that easily grew bored with meaningless pursuits. Although she loved to read on her own, Carie soon discovered that much of academia was less than inspiring. By the beginning of sophomore year, she had reached a motivational standstill.

One day in zoology class, while studying a species of worm called a nematode, she decided to drop out of college entirely. As an honors student, she was required to fill out a form to do so and state the reason for her withdrawal. The bookish Graves wrote down a quote from William Faulkner's *As I Lay Dying:* "We move with a motion so dream-like, so soporific, that it is as if time but not space were decreasing between it and us." The "it" for Carie was knowledge, and she felt she was not getting any closer to it.

For three months she just hung out with friends, then started working various jobs—selling Christmas trees, working the "graveyard" shift at Dunkin' Donuts—in order to save up for a trip to Europe. She had read James Michener's novel *The Drifters*, which detailed the wanderings of a group of youths in the '60s. Among other things, the book described miles of glistening, sandy beaches on an Italian coastline. That sounded like real life to Carie, far away from both her family farm and the theoretical confines of the university.

She was an attractive, nineteen-year-old American girl, hitchhiking around Europe alone. She had no real itinerary, no definite plan of action. For once, she wanted to take life as it came. Nights were spent in the open air or in youth hostels. Occasionally, she joined up with other travelers, like a fun-loving group of Japanese tourists, who drove her from France to northern Norway, singing old Elvis Presley songs. There she watched the midnight sun descend from the sky, briefly touch the ocean in a moment of red brilliance, and rise up again. Magically, here, there was no such thing as night.

Much of her trip was filled with this simple magic, but some of it was spent escaping from the unwanted attentions of older men. Her height and carefree American attitude were often mistaken for age and experience. In Sweden, a man invited her back to his house for dinner, introduced her to his wife and children, and then boldly propositioned her. Usually luck, not good judgment, kept her out of harm's way.

In Severn, Germany, she was picked up by a truck driver, who gave her cigarettes and cookies and generously showed her around the town. Toward the end of the day, when it was getting dark, her host began to drive her out of town, down a long dirt road. His broken English wasn't sufficient to describe where they were going, but it looked like they were headed for the countryside. Just as Carie began to get concerned, the road suddenly opened up to reveal a beautiful brick convent. She spent the night on a cot, safe among the nuns, and woke up surrounded by the majesty of the Black Forest. It was her twentieth birthday.

Still, despite the moments of beauty, Carie had begun to grow tired of traveling. She hitched a ride on a ferry from a fjord in Norway and rode it all the way to Florence, Italy, still in search of her Italian beach. Finally she thought she found it in the western coastal city of Livorno. Unfortunately, she had chosen an industrial port, with more aggressive Italian sailors than shimmering shores. She did find a beach, but it was covered with tar balls. She was running out of money and had a decision to make—go to France and pick grapes in September, or return home from her summer of wandering.

She had a long conversation with her brother, Ross, who urged her to come back to Madison and finish school. He had just completed his freshman year, and had rowed on a very successful frosh crew that had won the IRAs and even gone to Henley. Why didn't she try out for the fledgling women's team? Carie mulled over her brother's advice. She was weary of her aimless drifting, and the challenge of doing something with a single purpose appealed to her. Crew might be the very thing. In the journal that she had brought along with her on her trip, she wrote down two goals for the upcoming year. The first one was to go out for the women's crew.

Ironically, the prodigal daughter was returning home to engage in one of her father's favorite disciplines.

CARIE SHOWED UP for her first practice wearing one of her dad's betting shirts from the University of California. It was a cool, almost cocky, thing to do. In a sport that offered few rewards, betting shirts were the standard form of booty—either traded with another team, or wagered against them during a race. To wear a betting shirt meant that you had rowed and raced and probably beaten another team. The better the team, the higher the status of the shirt. And Cal had an excellent program.

At 6 feet 1 inch, Carie looked like a rower. She was the daughter of Robert Graves all right. But she hadn't won the tee shirt, *he* had. She hadn't even taken a stroke yet. She was overweight and smoked a pack of cigarettes every day. When the coach, Jay Mimier, sent the newcomers on a warm-up run, Carie could barely complete the mile-and-a-half loop. Whatever she had thought the betting shirt might do, it certainly didn't provide her with a new set of lungs.

She knew she was strong and she knew she was competitive. As a girl on the farm, she had often tested herself against the hired men, secretly competing with them as they shoveled grain and baled hay. But strength and size weren't enough. Looking around at the other novice recruits, Carie saw that she wasn't actually physically exceptional—there were other tall women and, surprisingly enough, two of them were also named Carie. In among the others, she suddenly felt normal, even ordinary. It was a strange feeling, both a comfort and a challenge.

Physically, Carie was very uncertain about herself. Was she strong? Yes, she thought she was. Was she beautiful? The European men had seemed to think so—but this, too, was a little unclear. Her height had always made her feel self-conscious around men. Sometimes, she'd meet a guy sitting down somewhere, like on a bus, and then be afraid to stand up. It bothered her to feel this way, so inhibited by her own body. In her journal, back in Livorno, Italy, the second goal she had chosen for herself was to model nude for the college art department. If she could stand naked in front of a group of strangers, she could stand up next to anyone fully clothed.

Besides, she needed another job, and modeling certainly paid better money than Dunkin' Donuts.

As crew practices progressed, so did the team runs, gradually lengthening to a distance of nine miles. Carie quickly realized that in addition to learning how to be skillful with an oar, she also had to build endurance. Even though crew racing often took place over short distances, the benefits of long-distance work were undisputed. During the fall, rowing's off-season, it was important to build an "endurance base" upon which shorter, more intense efforts could stand. In more physiological terms, such long, moderately paced aerobic workouts were the way to strengthen the cardiovascular system—the lungs that drew oxygen out of the air, the heart that pumped it, and the muscles that demanded it. A solid aerobic base could take months, if not years, to develop, and acquiring it could be very painful.

And so the first season was a difficult one, and for Carie, the focus every day was on pain—pain motivated by competitiveness, the need to distinguish herself among her teammates. The long training runs took the women far away from the Madison campus onto scenic farm roads, but for Carie these weren't pleasant jogs out in the countryside, where teammates would chat amiably and feel good about themselves. They were daily efforts to win against all comers. There was no talking, as this would have meant a less than full effort. She drove herself so hard on every run, in fact, that she began to fantasize about getting nicked by a car just to miss a day of practice.

Her first source of motivation was simply to be the best rower on the team, to win every challenge set in front of her. When she accomplished this, by the end of the fall, she realized that it wasn't sufficient—being the best couldn't accurately be measured against the rest of the team, or even against another team. Other people were false mirrors in which to view herself. Curiously, too, Carie's stake in rowing had very little to do with the aesthetics of technique or the enjoyment of being on the water, the obvious things that an outsider might identify as the inspirations of rowing. In a way, these were just distractions to her and the intense game she began to play against herself when she took an oar into her hands.

Yet along with the pain, Carie felt a great elation, a pure joy from the simple motion of pulling on an oar as hard as she could. It was hard to explain to those who didn't row, but it had to do with the feeling of being absorbed in the rowing motion, and the direct connection it provided to her inner being. To know yourself truly involved going up against yourself—confronting the demons of doubt and weakness within and defeating them by sheer force of will. It was this that made the pain involved negotiable, and provided her with a sense of power and control that had been so absent in her life.

T w o

G AIL PIERSON WALKED SLOWLY along the narrow floating dock, with the careful step of balanced burden. The long wooden boat that rested heavily on her head was double-tapered like a shield to the morning sky, and her arms—slightly forward and off to each side—held the metal riggers to form a stable tripod with her head. The dock shifted unsteadily as she moved along its length, forcing her to walk flat-footed and loose-jointed, like a sailor. It was wet and cold with April dew that she felt through her wool socks as she stopped and toed for the edge.

Deftly, she rolled the shell off her head, bending down to place it carefully on the water. Morning mist was still rising off the surface of the river, and it left the water flat and still thick in sleep. Her boat lay on it like an autumn leaf, not yet breaking the surface tension.

She quickly fit the oars into the swivel locks and clamped the brass gates around their leather collars. It was a brand-new boat, a German-made Empacher, and Gail Pierson was quite proud of it. Twenty-six feet long and less than ten inches wide, it weighed thirty-four pounds without the shoes. The inner framework was of

Sitka spruce, a wood that possessed remarkable strength and yet was extremely light in weight. The outer skin was a honey-colored, Honduras mahogany—barely an eighth of an inch thick. Everything about the boat was delicate and beautiful—yet strong and fast in the right hands.

With her right foot she stepped into the center of the boat, the only place that could support her full weight of 145 pounds. She was 5 feet 8 inches, not very big for a sweep rower, but certainly adequate for a single sculler. Scullers relied on finesse more than sheer force, and even their equipment looked more refined. Gail's boat was so narrow that she needed to use the oars for stability as she gingerly stepped into it, extending her port oar out onto the water and laying the starboard oar out over the dock. If you didn't do this, the shell would quickly flip over when you tried to sit down, behaving like a wild horse that didn't want to be ridden. Balancing briefly on one leg, she gathered both oar handles into her right hand like reins and carefully lowered herself into the tiny cockpit.

Cradling the oar handles in her lap, she slid her feet into a pair of Adidas track cleats. The shoes were bolted onto a wooden foot board in the stern of the boat, and were the only thing that anchored her firmly to it. She rolled back on the sliding seat to test it once, to make sure it didn't need oiling. A squeaky seat could ruin the silent pleasure of a row. Then, taking the oar handles into her right hand again, she shoved off with the left to clear away from the dock. The motion sent small waves across the water.

It felt good to be alone, in her single scull again, after a previous morning spent trying to row in the eight with seven other women, followed around by a reporter from *Sports Illustrated*. She had not gotten a good workout with him dogging her heels, snapping photographs and asking questions about her life on and off the water.

She began rowing with just her arms, then added her back and legs, taking quarter, then half, and finally full strokes; lengthening out, stretching her calves and back, her blades entering the water without much effort. The delicate scull glided smoothly and silently forward, with the puddles of the oars yawning out in pairs behind her. As she paddled upstream, waking the water, she knew that soon she would be one of the only ones on the river. Everyone else in Boston had normal lives to go to, most locked inside the huge office buildings that she saw from her scull on the downstream horizon of the Charles River. It was nice to have the water all to herself, to be momentarily free from her own responsibilities at the university.

She always felt good pulling away from the dock, leaving her work shoes sitting there idle. One of the more amusing stories she had told the reporter the day before was how she had once returned from an afternoon row to find her shoes missing. Frantically, she had searched the boathouse for them. She was going to be late for class. Finally she concluded that someone had either taken them by mistake or they'd fallen in the river, so she gave up her search and grabbed an old pair of size-thirteen men's sneakers. When she showed up to teach her economics class, the undergraduates at MIT had regarded her with bemused silence. But it hadn't been the first time that people had looked at her strangely.

The reporter had been a nice enough fellow, but like most journalists who knew little about rowing, he had needed to get a bead on it, and on her, in short order to meet a deadline and keep within a limited word count imposed by some harried editor. She didn't and couldn't tell him everything about either subject. It would take too long, and he didn't have the time. You had to be guarded with reporters as a female athlete, too, and not come off sounding too strong or too masculine. They were threatened if you did that, and immediately labeled you as something less than a real woman.

She headed upstream, towards a little section above Eliot Bridge where she'd measured a straight, 500-meter course for herself, pacing it off over the ice one winter. She automatically checked her hands to make sure they were positioned correctly. Compared to sweep oars, which took two hands to use, sculls were small and light, and required more finesse. Your hands had to overlap, left over right, so they wouldn't collide with one another during the middle of the stroke. She had mastered this, as well as all the many other subtle elements of technique required to keep a single from flipping, to keep it moving forward smoothly. Everything you did with your hands affected the oars, and everything the oars did affected the balance and the glide.

When you sculled well, it looked deceptively simple and effortless—boat and oars and athlete as one motion. After five years, Gail Pierson had learned how to make it look easy enough, especially to some outsider who didn't know much about the sport. She had also learned how to handle reporters, to appear relaxed and natural, and yet to be careful about what she said. You didn't tell everything directly, you let them draw the information out of you, and let them believe they had discovered it all by themselves.

Her age and education helped, combined with her winsome smile and simple bearing. She kept her straight blonde hair cut short, to keep it out of the way, her hands and body free of jewelry. She had a flat, matter-of-fact intonation to her voice, softened by a slight Louisiana drawl. The down-home voice, and her no-nonsense way of putting things, had a way of disarming most reporters even after they'd learned about the PhD in economics and four national championship victories in doubles trap shooting. She was a handsome, well-educated woman, not someone you could dismiss as young and cute.

Another reporter from *Sports Illustrated* had covered the 1974 Head of the Charles Regatta the previous fall, and had written about the women's races with a trace of subtle but deprecating humor that was all too typical of the kind of coverage they received. After a brief sketch of Pierson and her victory in the women's singles race, as well as mention of a Radcliffe junior named Wiki Royden, who had placed second, he had shifted his focus onto a non-competitive sculler from Wellesley and made her into an amusing, clownish figure. Apparently, she had named her boat the *J. Alfred Prufrock*, and had recited the T. S. Eliot poem "dreamily" up the course. He described, in a little too much detail, how another rower had hit her in the stomach with an oar, and how, when her bandanna had fallen off into the Charles, she had reached for it and flipped over.

Well, at least it was coverage.

The sun was high over the river now, and as Gail rowed upstream she passed a few college crews out practicing for their spring season: Boston University, MIT, Harvard University and its sister school, Radcliffe. The Charles River was definitely starting to get more crowded now, especially with the addition of the women's teams. Only a few years ago, there had been none at all, and Gail knew she was responsible for at least some of the change. It was one of the reasons why the reporter had come.

As the crews went, they broke up the surface of the river into a mosaic of greens and blues, reflections of the trees and sky above. It was no longer a dull brown, but a brilliant pastiche of color. She looked back at the puddles that her own strokes had created, which sparkled as they drew the sun's light into them. Her gaze drifted back past the path of whirlpools, swirling inward and below. Sweat broke and cooled on her brow, and soon she was no longer conscious of the rowing, just the feel of the water and the memories it contained—some of which she had told the reporter, and some of which she had not.

She had told him how she had taken up rowing by happenstance, in 1969, not long after she had arrived in Cambridge to teach at Harvard. She had not told him how she had ended up on the Charles partly to replace one of her other athletic loves, swimming, which she found rather difficult to do at the university. Harvard had only recently gone coed, and some facilities were still segregated into the two institutions known as Harvard and Radcliffe colleges. Only men swam in the main campus pool—

unencumbered by swimsuits. When Gail was ushered to a tiny pool on the Radcliffe campus, she was greatly disheartened. While she had been earning her PhD at the University of Michigan, she had swum laps almost every day in the Olympic-sized pool there and found it an effective way to relieve the stress of academia. The Radcliffe pool was clearly insufficient.

The Harvard economics department was anxious to please their very first female professor, a fact unknown to Gail herself when she accepted the two-year junior post. She had come to Harvard via Michigan, to see how things worked in the East. Originally from the small rural town of Natchitoches, Louisiana, she found the academic community in Cambridge stimulating, but yearned for a sense of the outdoors. Since her focus in economics was mostly on the theoretical, she needed to balance it with a connection to the physical world.

Seeing her dismay at the swimming pool situation, Arthur Smithies, a senior member of the faculty, suggested that she take up rowing. He was a member of the Cambridge Boat Club, a private rowing and social club, and would be happy to bring Gail along as a guest. Gail liked most activities having to do with water, and readily accepted the invitation. She had also taken up sailing in Michigan, and even bought herself a 505 racing boat. But again, in Boston, sailing was a difficult proposition. All the serious yachting took place in Marblehead—a forty-minute drive from Cambridge. And the cottagey-looking Cambridge Boat Club was just a stone's throw from the Harvard campus.

She took to sculling as she had taken to swimming and sailing; in a way it combined the attributes of both. It allowed the rhythmic, repetitive motion of swimming, which strengthened the muscles and the heart. It also allowed some of the tactical boat maneuvering of sailing. She enjoyed being out on the Charles River, which was one of the few natural havens someone from the country could retreat to in the middle of a busy place like Boston. Once she had gotten out on the water, the city seemed to disappear, and she was transported for a few hours to a completely different world. Like many other urban rivers, the Charles wasn't especially clean, but it did feed many species of trees and shrubs along its banks, and it was a viable home to ducks, geese, and other waterfowl.

The cold, pre-dawn drill reminded Gail of her hunting days, when she and her father would wake up at 4:00 A.M. and row out to the duck blinds, small huts that stood on pilings near the shore. She had enjoyed talking to her dad, waiting for the birds; it made the cold and the dark more bearable.

She had told the reporter a little about hunting, but not how she had obtained her first gun at age seven, a "32 Special" Winchester rifle. Her father had taken her to a local fair, and Gail had tried her luck at a dart-throwing booth. Already exhibiting an uncanny sense of aim that would soon carry over into her shooting, Gail punctured the requisite number of balloons to win a prize. There were several choices to appeal to the wide range of potential winners, and the man behind the booth encouraged her toward a teddy bear—a suitable gift for a seven-year-old girl. But reviewing the prizes with her father, Gail had a sense that the rifle was special—maybe to her, maybe to him, maybe to both of them. She made her choice.

When the man in the balloon booth began to protest—a rifle simply wasn't appropriate for a young girl—Gail's father had quarreled with him, and then fetched the police. In the end, the gun was hers. She would never forget the incident with her father, for it marked the beginning of their hunting days together. Will Pierson had one daughter already, and had been hoping for a son, someone he could take hunting and fishing. But Gail's older sister, Elise, was more of a traditional girl (she would end up getting married by age seventeen and having five children); she certainly had no interest in such things.

Gail, however, was a different matter.

If Will Pierson had wanted a son to go hunting with, he soon found a willing and gifted companion in his younger daughter. They began with dove shooting on the local farms around Natchitoches and Shreveport. Dove shoots were a social gathering of sorts, with fifty or more participants, including many families. Typically, a big barbecue would be held on someone's property, and then the shooting would begin. The small gray birds were incredibly fast. And as they winged their way in and out of the cornfields, it took a keen eye and quick reflexes to bring one down. Gail was only ten years old then, and while perhaps not the only girl with a gun, certainly the only crack shot. Her shooting ability was so exceptional that she was frequently sequestered by some of the older men who couldn't make their quota. Only ten birds were allowed per man, but another hunter could help you gain your limit—even if it *was* a ten-year-old girl.

Duck hunting came next, further afield. When she was old enough, she was taken on a four-day trip to her father's hunting cabin on the Tensas River. In the pre-dawn darkness, waiting for the ducks, she would listen to the low voices of the other men, telling their stories and problems to one another with an openness that seldom occurred at home. The young girl may have seemed invisible to them, but Gail was listening all along.

Now, some twenty years later, she was looking at water birds from her single scull instead of a duck blind. The mallards that floated lazily on the Charles River seemed like an entirely different breed, citified birds that were too lazy or too stupid to move when her scull suddenly came upon them. Most likely, the ducks didn't know what to make of a scull, which spent half its time on water and half on land, just like them, but didn't behave like a proper water bird. It was forever beating its ungainly wings, but could never seem to lift off into the air. Instead it just plowed its way rudely up and down the river, barely looking where it was going.

Initially, while she was learning how to scull, Gail indeed looked clumsy in a boat and felt rather foolish, splashing and crashing her way up the winding river, which was full of bridges and other obstacles. A few times she even flipped the delicate, narrow boat, after placing an oar in the water the wrong way. After several weeks, however, using the same diligence she applied to other sports, she was moving the wooden boat quickly and quietly enough to surprise a few ducks that weren't paying attention—swatting them playfully with the back of her oar blade. Well, it wasn't quite as good as hunting, but it would have to do.

Still, something was lacking from her forays on the river, and it had nothing to do with ducks. She'd tried to excel at everything she did, but it was hard to do this out on the river alone, hard to gauge one's progress.

In shooting there had been an organization, a means to compete. As Gail got into her teens, she took her hunting skills and put them to work first skeet and then trap shooting. It wasn't real hunting, but it was fun and quite profitable. Trap shooting was even more difficult than skeet, because you didn't know where the targets would come from. Under the tutelage of the great Mercer Tennille, she'd quickly become a champion doubles trap shooter. Doubles didn't mean two people shooting together, as in tennis or rowing. It meant one person simultaneously shooting at two clay pigeons, which took unpredictable paths. She was Louisiana state champion twice, against both women and men, and ranked as one of the top all-around shooters in the country. While she was in college, the cash prizes had actually helped put her through school.

There wasn't much interest in hunting in Massachusetts, she told the reporter, who was amused by the "Ducks Unlimited" sticker he spotted in the back window of her old Mercury Cougar. Naturally, he wanted to get a photo of Gail shooting her gun—the Annie Oakley angle.

There was no money in rowing, she told him, but that didn't really matter. Gail didn't need the money so much anymore, but what she still craved was the physical challenge that the classroom didn't offer. She was an MIT professor now, and could earn her living talking about monetary theory and interest rates. But part of her still yearned to be competitive, to be the hunter, and it continued to come through in whatever she did. Sculling wasn't going to be any different. And if there was no place to get a prize, she'd just have to create one.

Fortunately, after a few months of figuring out how to scull on the Charles, Gail was taken in by a small group of competitive male scullers who trained together every morning. It happened unceremoniously, in much the same way as her childhood hunting experience. There she had also enjoyed the company of keen sportsmen. And now the sculling fraternity quickly recognized in her the signs of a fellow enthusiast—like her willingness to wake up before sunrise every morning and cover most of the ten-mile length of the Charles that began at the locks bounding Boston Harbor and ended in a small waterfall at Watertown Square.

Among the group was Bob Arlett, a painfully shy and talented sculler who often could not even bring himself to coach Gail directly. He was too embarrassed to describe certain aspects of sculling technique, which often needed to be rendered in graphic detail. He had to have another sculler, Mike Fredericks, tell Gail that her upper body should remain relaxed in sculling, to imagine that she had "balls of axle grease under her armpits." There were Ben Jones and Paul Wilson, a highly acclaimed local sculler who had stroked an intramural Harvard crew to victory at England's Henley Royal Regatta. And later, of course, there was Sy Cromwell, who had actually won the Diamond Sculls at Henley in 1964, and had won an Olympic silver medal in the double. But Sy was special.

Sy was actually Seymour Cromwell II, the grandson of a former president of the New York Stock Exchange. His mother was a descendant of Phillip Livingston, one of the signers of the Declaration of Independence. Sy had once joked with Gail about their different backgrounds, pointing out that her relatives may have *come* from Louisiana, but his ancestors had *bought* it. But aside from private jokes like this, he was a big, gentle man who was decidedly low-key. If anything, he made an effort to hide his privileged background, and had swapped the name Seymour for the simpler Sy.

They'd met one morning out on the river, when their two sculls nearly collided in mid-stream. It was somewhere near the finish line of the Head of the Charles, and Gail was racing upstream at full tilt, chasing a pack of male scullers. Sy was heading downstream, back to Riverside Boat Club, and neither one of them was really looking where they were going. When they turned around suddenly and saw one another, there was barely enough time for them to avert a crash by digging their blades down into the water and using them as crude brakes. The two sculls slowed and then slid together in a rather clumsy embrace, with Gail's port oar draped over Sy's bow, and his resting over the top of her stern. But instead of cursing defensively at one another, the two scullers carefully disentangled and proceeded to make awkward introductions. The next day, Sy showed up at the Cambridge Boat Club to make sure that Gail and her boat were all right. It was the first of many such visits on his part. Some of the men in Gail's training group secretly whispered that she had purposely run her scull into Sy Cromwell just to meet him. As for Sy, he now took a keen interest in the woman whom fate had chosen to place in his path. In any case, it was an auspicious start to a long-standing courtship.

He proposed to her two years later, in 1972, but was reluctant to actually get married because he didn't have a "serious" job at the time. Gail was a professor at MIT and Sy was teaching at Groton. He had a problem shucking off the old concept of the male as the financial supporter, the female as the nurturer. But it was Sy who had the real gift of nurturing people. He could get into a group of big egos and immediately smooth out all the individual hang-ups and tensions. Just by sitting down and talking with someone he could soon have them laughing and making light of their problems. It was a natural gift, and it made him a good teacher and coach. It also made people want to be around him.

When the reporter had wanted to get a photograph of Gail and her gun, Sy had taken them out to Groton where he taught preparatory school, and they'd almost gotten arrested for discharging a firearm on private property. Gail held the rifle while Sy threw the clay pigeons, and when the photographer took a picture of them together, Gail was quick to mention that they were "just good friends." Later that evening, she added, they were going to the opera. If you didn't have a boyfriend or husband, that was suspicious; female athletes were often labeled and dismissed as lesbians. But Gail didn't want anyone to think she was promiscuous, either—especially her mother, who read everything written about her.

SINGLE SCULLERS were an odd lot, even in the peculiar world of rowing. They were both revered and distrusted by other rowers—revered because sculling was a higher form of rowing art, much harder to learn than the "sweep" rowing done at colleges. In their narrow, feather-light boats, scullers had to develop a much greater sensitivity to balance and finesse. They also had to control everything in the boat, including the steering, whereas a team rower could just blend in to the overall motion of the boat, leave the driving to the coxswain and the stroke rating to the oarsman known as the stroke. A sculler had to be helmsman, stroke, and rower all wrapped into one, more like the pilot of a small plane than a passenger on a big one.

If there was an underlying distrust of single scullers, it stemmed from the fact that most tended to be strong individualists, highly opinionated on any aspect of rowing. Since a sculler by necessity had to think about almost everything related to technique, training, or rigging, she had an immediate, experiential basis of knowledge that was often difficult to refute. It was hard to say whether this opinionated behavior came from being alone in a boat for long periods of time, and having to learn the art of rowing almost single-handedly, or whether these unusual circumstances ensured that those who took to the sport would by necessity be individualistic types.

Years later, Gail would conclude that single scullers were outcasts in the world of rowing, frequently the ones who couldn't stand being coached or weren't very tolerant of rowing in the same boat with others.

There was also a historic precedent for distrusting single scullers. During the heyday of American rowing in the late nineteenth century, scullers had been the ones who had corrupted the sport, who engaged in prize races that led to crooked gambling practices. Back then, single scullers were the sports icons of the day, men like Charles Courtney from Ithaca, New York, and Edward "The Boy in Blue" Hanlan from Toronto. A top-ranked single sculler could draw a crowd of 30,000 spectators and make a small fortune in prize money. A few of these races took place right in Boston, including one that ended in tragedy with a train accident that killed the local favorite, Patsy Reagan. But then the gambling had appeared and made the outcome of these races more and more suspect; accidents began to happen that were obviously staged.

In 1872, amateur rowing rules were put in place by a newly created organization known as the National Association of Amateur Oarsmen (NAAO). The rules sought to eliminate the corruption of commercialism and ensure that rowing would take place for rowing's sake. Money led to corruption and "dirty tricks," and rowing needed to remain pure. From this time on, no amateur competitor could make a living at the sport of rowing or derive any pecuniary benefit from it. An amateur was one who rowed "for pleasure or recreation only, and during his leisure hours," who did not "abandon or neglect his usual business or occupation for the purpose of training."

Because of this, Gail Pierson and Sy Cromwell could never be pros, could never make a cent from their skill with a pair of oars.

In the States, at least, the amateur rule had good intentions. In England, unfortunately, it took on a classist form of prejudice—amateurs there could not work in any trade in which they used their hands. Jack Kelly, the famous American sculler, had been denied the opportunity to compete at the Henley Royal Regatta because he had been a bricklayer. And just as there had been rules against the working class then, Gail soon discovered there was an unwritten code against female competitors now.

The men in her training group had talked excitedly about the thrill of racing, especially in the local fall race, the Head of the Charles Regatta. Why didn't Gail enter? they suggested. The Head of the Charles was an informal, three-mile row against the clock, attended by the local universities and private rowing clubs whose boathouses lined the banks of the tea-colored river. As a fall race, patterned after the "Head of the River" race in England, it was designed to promote rowing during the off-season of the sport and provide a festive outdoor event for all of Boston to see.

Even though she'd only been sculling for about five months, she eagerly agreed and began to fill out an entry form. There was only one problem—there were no women's events.

The very first year the regatta had been held, in 1965, two women's crews from a program called the Philadelphia Girls Rowing Club were invited to Boston and did compete against each other. But that was four years ago, and no further interest had been shown in women's events. No woman had *ever* raced a single before. There were a handful of other women who sculled in New England, and sometimes even raced, but competitive rowing was by and large a man's game. Locally, there were men's crew teams at Harvard, MIT, Northeastern, and Boston University—and at the three private clubs: Union, Riverside, and the Cambridge Boat Club, who sponsored the race.

The reason for this was largely cultural, tied to the ideal of "womanhood" perfected in the 1950s. Rowing built male character, muscle, and fraternal ties that might later on prove important in the worlds of commerce, politics, and war. What use did a woman have for these? Teddy Roosevelt had rowed, and so had his cousin Franklin, both while they had attended Harvard College. Although rowing might no longer enjoy a popular audience, oarsmen often had influence that extended into powerful political circles. Women's rowing had actually existed at local colleges like Wellesley since the late 1800s, and some racing had been held, but these were intrasquad competitions that were often judged on the basis of style—not power and raw speed.

Gail looked closely at the application to the Head of the Charles Regatta again. Although there were no women's events, she saw no place where it said a woman *couldn't* enter.

T h r e e

IN ORDER TO UNDERSTAND competitive rowing, you first had to understand pain. Not the common, ordinary sort that visits most people on an occasional basis—back pain, headaches, even broken bones. These are all valid forms of pain that can challenge an individual's patience and sanity. And rowing, Carie Graves quickly discovered, certainly offered its share of these—the blistered hands that never quite healed, that had to be carefully monitored lest they get infected from being constantly ground into the rough, grimy oar handle; the sore muscles over the entire body; the occasional rib and back injuries. But the real pain of rowing, the one required for a racing effort, was far more internal and intense.

First, it was a self-inflicted pain, completely unnecessary for someone to undergo. Second, because everyone in the crew had to be equally committed during a race and could not slack off, it often reached an intensity that went beyond the limits of the individual rowers. This factor could sometimes cause a rower to black out and slump unconscious over the oar at the end of a race.

Physiologically, this pain stems from the simple fact that, during a race, the rower's body can't get enough oxygen to run efficiently. For ordinary exertion, the body simply employs its "aerobic" or oxygen-using process, which allows the body to take in oxygen, transfer it to the bloodstream, and distribute it throughout the body. Red blood cells ferry the oxygen from the lungs to the muscles, and remove waste in the form of carbon dioxide.

But when the muscles are used intensely for an extended period of time, the system fails to work so well. Two detrimental things happen, creating a vicious cycle that disables the normal aerobic process. First, less oxygen is available for the muscles, despite increased efforts by the heart to pump blood faster. Second, metabolic waste begins to collect in the muscles.

From the outside, the overtaxed rower looks like a fish out of water, desperately gasping for more breath. Internally, however, it is the buildup of metabolic waste in the muscles that causes the most amount of pain. In rowing, generally the legs, or the quadriceps, feel it the most—a sharp, burning sensation that some rowers describe as being stabbed with a dull knife.

Carie and her novice teammates, of course, weren't aware of this scientific explanation for their pain; they simply wanted to see how far they could push themselves. Aside from running, the other device used to measure such an intense effort was called the ergometer—a huge, metal rowing simulator that looked like a medieval torture device. The ergometer was dreaded by most rowers, partly because you didn't go anywhere by rowing it and didn't move anything except a little needle on a meter, which registered your efforts with supreme indifference.

For Carie, however, the erg was a purer vehicle for her confrontations with pain, which were providing her with a somewhat Nietzschean notion of self-worth. (To give in to pain was to compromise oneself; to push through it was to emerge more pure.) Her goal was to row hard enough to nearly pass out during every piece. Her passion was contagious. Other novice teammates tried to emulate Carie, driving each other toward greater and greater efforts. In its newness, it was like a game to them, an unexplored territory that existed deep within. What were their ultimate limits?

The competitiveness of the new novice squad caused several veteran rowers to quit. By the spring, only three or four remained. Carie was put in the six seat of the varsity boat for her first racing season, which consisted of a dual race against the University of Minnesota and then the Nationals in California. Unfortunately, there simply weren't that many women's crews in the country in 1974, and fewer still in the Midwest. The race against Minnesota was held on Lake Elmo in St. Paul. It was an 800-meter sprint held in thundershowers. For Carie, who kept her head down all the way, it was a terrifying experience. When the race was over and she finally looked up, however, she saw that they had won by a substantial margin.

Perhaps this crew racing was an easy business after all, she thought. But during their next race, the Nationals, held on Lake Merritt in Oakland that spring, the varsity did not even make the finals. What did it all mean? Were they a good team or a bad team?

With little competition to test them, the power and intensity of the Wisconsin squad came from within. In a sense, their isolation may have been a blessing in disguise, for it allowed them to develop to their own potential. On the one hand, having other crews around might have provided a "reality check" to see how fast they were going. On the other hand, especially with a crew as young as this, excessive competition might have been a distraction and hampered the focus that had to develop within the boat. It was this inner focus, cohesiveness, and trust that needed to be solidly in place for a crew to succeed. That, and the inherent desire to win.

Certainly, other things won crew races besides physical and mental toughness. A good coxswain, for example, to steer a straight course. A capable person in the stroke seat, who could pace the efforts of the others and know when to take the stroke rating up and down. A good boat, which would not be fifty pounds heavier than the one the other team was using. These were issues that the coach took care of, while the athletes were just supposed to put their heads down and pull hard. Ultimately, too, it was the coach who put the racing season into its proper perspective and let the rowers know what they needed to work on.

Jay Mimier, Carie's coach, thought about all of these things over the summer, and came back the next fall ready to make some changes. In many ways, Mimier was like a lot of other crew coaches, a former Wisco rower who had been practically drafted into service. Two years earlier, the freshman men's coach, Doug O'Neal, had asked him to help out, unprepared for the flood of women interested in joining the new program. The women's coaching position paid $500, compared to about $5000 for the men. "It sounds like good beer money," joked the good-natured Mimier. He was completing his law degree, and thought that coaching might be an excellent way to put some of his knowledge of rowing to the test.

Before law school, Mimier had been a national team oarsman, coached by Harvard's famed Harry Parker and the noteworthy Cal coach Steve Gladstone. Few oarsmen achieved this level of excellence, and fewer still could walk away from it all, cold turkey. Rowing was still in Mimier's blood, and it didn't matter to him that he would be coaching a group of women who had little or no idea about the sport.

He had enjoyed Harry Parker's way of coaching, a minimalist style that was non-intrusive to the natural development of a crew. One of the key tenets to this method, it seemed, was to first identify the stroke of the crew, the person everyone else could follow. Once you found the right stroke, everything else would fall into place. But a good one was not always so easy to identify. Ideally, the stroke was someone with a sense of rhythm and good technique. Most important, however, it was someone the rest of the team could put their entire confidence in when the chips were down.

Mimier had his eye on Carie Graves, but he had a few misgivings. She *was* the strongest, if not the smoothest, rower in the boat. And her ability to lead was undeniable. He couldn't help but notice the way the other rowers looked up to her in awe as she drove herself incredibly hard on every workout, on every stroke. She didn't have the smoothest technique in the boat, but she did have a quick catch and didn't waste any time getting her oar through the water. Besides, the stroke from the year before, Carol Milner, had sustained a rib injury and couldn't pull with the intensity needed to lead the crew.

His reluctance, if anything, was more related to her character. If at times she acted the role of a born leader, she could also be impatient with anyone less able or willing to do what she could do. Even though the stroke led the rest of the crew, they also had to sense what everyone else could handle—and that was an acquired skill that came with maturity. Carie was an individual who rowed purely from inside her own head, and had an almost self-righteous attitude about what was good for the boat.

Mimier noticed this big-headed behavior start to emerge as soon as he put her in at stroke. Sometimes, she had heated discussions with the coxswain about when to encourage the crew and when to shut up. She would even take it upon herself to school a new candidate on how to use the rudder, how to steer only when the blades were in the water so as not to throw off the delicate balance of the boat. Mimier was having trouble finding good coxswains that autumn, and Carie was making it even harder—no one wanted to sit facing her. He might find a good prospect, one crazy enough to wake up at 5:30 A.M. and brave the cold waters of Lake Mendota, but few survived the hazing of the new stroke.

Still, even if she wasn't the ideal candidate, Carie did seem to bring the boat together. That, in the end, was the ultimate goal. Another advantage of placing her at stroke, Mimier figured, was to put her cockiness to the test. To a great extent, the stroke carried the weight of the team's success on her shoulders. Either they would all indeed rise to her level of intensity, or she would drive them into the ground and learn an important lesson about teamwork. Even a stroke had to be in tune with the rest of the crew, had to have eyes in the back of her head.

For this reason, not everyone liked to stroke. But from Carie's perspective, it was the perfect seat for her. She felt more in control there and better able to communicate with the coxswain how much she wanted to win. Generally, no talking was permitted in a crew, aside from the coxswain, but the stroke and the cox could often work together in a joint effort to make the boat go fast. The coxswain could see the overall picture in front of her—whose blade was going in the water out of synch with the others, for example—but the stroke could sometimes have a better sense of the ideal rhythm and power the crew needed to move the shell, depending on where they were in a race and the water conditions.

Carie had other reasons for wanting to lead the varsity crew: she wanted to set the limits for how hard they worked. While most of the women in the boat were hoping just to make the team and have a good season, Carie was already looking much further ahead. Recently, she'd read somewhere that the 1976 Olympics would be the first to include women's crew. Although she was only a junior now, when Carie heard this news she had an immediate premonition that she would be on that team. The first step was to make the 1975 national team, which, as rumor had it, would be coached by Harvard's Harry Parker himself.

F o u r

WHEN GAIL PIERSON HEARD THE NEWS about the women's Olympic event, she was on a train headed out of Hanover, Germany. She had just finished racing in a U.S. quadrascull at the 1972 World Championships with some women from Long Beach. Things hadn't gone all that well for her boat. The Europeans were very strong in rowing, particularly sculling, and Gail had found out firsthand just how difficult it was to beat them. She'd finally gotten her wish, however, to compete at the top level of the sport—only three years after entering her first sculling race, on the Charles River. But in Boston she had only needed to convince a few men to let her compete. Getting to the World Championships had turned out to be a much harder task.

Each woman in the quadrascull had needed to pay her own way, even make her own uniform, and they had no official coach—just Gail's fiancé from Cambridge, Sy Cromwell. They'd had to borrow an old, clunky boat, and were no match for the nationally sponsored teams from countries like Russia and Germany—countries that actually paid their female athletes to train. Not only did the

U.S. group have no financial support, but also they had been given bad information from the start.

The strongest memory from the trip was not of the racing, in fact, but of standing in a train station somewhere in Germany, waiting for some government official to verify who they were and why they were even there. The U.S. rowing overseers hadn't even told their German hosts that a group of American women was coming over to compete. They had assured Gail and the rest of the squad that they didn't need visas to enter the country.

If only things had gone as easily as they had in Boston, when Gail had first competed in the Head of the Charles Regatta. That year, because no woman had ever entered the singles race before, the race directors had simply put her into the men's event. She beat a half-dozen of the male scullers, but that didn't phase her much. After all, she'd bested men many times before, in various shooting competitions. There was a real skill involved with rowing, just as there was in shooting. But there was also a certain amount of power needed to do well—both physical and political.

Most of the men she beat didn't seem to mind too much—at least they didn't try to force her off the course as they had done to Kathrine Switzer, the first woman to run the Boston Marathon in 1967. What Gail had learned about men early on was that, ultimately, they respected results. Despite how they might initially gripe and protest, once you'd proven yourself to them physically, the doubts either ceased or at least became less pronounced.

After Gail rowed in that first Head, she persuaded the race committee to create a women's event, to be held annually if enough interest could be sustained. Every year thereafter, the interest in it had exploded, and Gail had become the acknowledged leader—a Pied Piper guiding the small band of women over the twisting, turning upstream course that was full of obstacles: bridges, buoys, and other boats. One year she even flipped when a fishing boat backed right into her—unaware or unconcerned that a regatta was going on. But then, an even stranger thing had happened. Instead of rowing past Gail's overturned boat, the rest of the women in the event stopped rowing and waited for Gail to right herself. Then they all resumed the race.

As she began to enter a few other races around the country, she thought it was unfortunate that more women weren't rowing competitively. Most women, she observed, had never been trained to be competitive in anything but getting a man, never put their hearts and souls into anything but having a family. That, she thought, would hurt them in sports, especially in team sports, where cooperation was necessary.

The little incident on the Charles was promising indeed, and it was nice to have the local event as a women's showcase. Winning the Head of the Charles, however, was not enough. More women should be racing nationally and internationally, she decided, just like the U.S. men's teams that went to the World Championships and the Olympics. And when Gail expressed some of these thoughts to a group of other women rowers at the 1972 Nationals in Seattle, they elected her president of the National Women's Rowing Association (the NWRA). That's where the trip to Germany had been hatched. If a group of them could form a team, she thought, perhaps they could make some real headway in the sport.

Of course the idea had occurred to others before.

In 1967, a group of Philadelphia oarswomen led by Ernestine Bayer had paid their own way to the European Championships held in Vichy, France. The Europeans had welcomed the American entry, but the U.S. rowing officials had almost forbidden them to race. A few years later a like-minded group from Lake Washington Rowing Club had done the same, and then came Gail's group in the quadrascull. Rowing in old, borrowed boats, these women's teams had all performed unremarkably, demonstrating what the naysayers had said all along: American women weren't ready to compete at the Worlds, or the Olympics.

One of the biggest problems, Gail discovered, was that the

men holding the purse strings and running the events had not allowed women much quarter, had not thought they were competitive enough to face off against the Europeans. The U.S. actually had an organization, the National Rowing Federation (NRF), that helped fund men's rowing during non-Olympic years, so that they could compete at the European and World Championships. Prior to their departure for Germany, Gail had written to Bud Smith, the head of the NRF, and he had sent her a check for $450 to help defray some of the traveling expenses for the band of four women and their coxswain. Gail promptly sent it back with a short note, indicating that the amount was too small.

But after their race in Germany, riding back on the train, they had gotten the good news. Gail was scanning a German newspaper and thought she read that women's rowing had just been approved to be included in the next Olympic Games. Her four teammates thought she was crazy, but when one of them got out their German dictionary, they discovered that her translation was indeed correct. And that, in itself, was cause for celebration.

Back in Boston, she wrote again to Bud Smith, asking for more money, and he responded by saying that any women's team that wanted funding would need to fulfill a minimum time-standard requirement—to clock a certain time over a set racing distance. She agreed with this in principle, but also realized as an economist that any new venture required a certain amount of capital. Money was needed to get women's rowing off the ground, not only to pay for things like uniforms and good equipment, but also to instill the confidence that came along with such support. And so she worked for this behind the scenes.

Without telling the U.S. rowing organizations, the NRF and the NAAO, she petitioned the Olympic Committee to create a separate board for women's rowing with a budget of its own. After all, U.S. swimming and track and field had their own women's branches, why shouldn't crew? That way, Gail correctly reasoned, the U.S. rowing groups that had been so stingy in the past would never even get their hands on the Olympic funds and delegate which teams were more deserving of it. She got her wish, and the WORC was created—the Women's Olympic Rowing Committee.

Once the Olympic decision had been made in 1972, things got easier. On the collegiate level, too, things had begun to happen. That same year, a federal law called Title IX had been passed, which required American universities to dispense funds equally to men's and women's sports teams. With proper funding, women's crew programs all around the country were able to start purchasing some quality equipment and entice good coaches. Now, on both the collegiate and the club level, women's rowing was really starting to grow.

In 1973, several U.S. women's crews, a mixture of college and club teams, made the imposed time standard and secured funds for a trip to the World Championships in Moscow. A full complement of female rowers was sent, including an eight from Radcliffe, a quadrascull, a double, and a single sculler named Joan Lind, who had rowed in the '72 quad with Gail. Not only that, but they traveled with the men's team, fully recognized. Lind was one of the Long Beach group, and when she surprised everyone by getting a silver medal in Moscow, the first international medal for U.S. women, they truly began to get respect. The next year, two Princeton women rowing a pair made the finals. Things were getting better, there was talent out there, it just needed to be harnessed. They still needed a coach and a place to train. And they needed more respect.

Making women's rowing socially acceptable was as much of a challenge as getting appropriate funding and physical resources. Another part of her mission as president of the NWRA, Gail discovered, lay in educating the younger generation of women who were the beneficiaries of the Olympic decision and the Title IX legislation. And so, when she was invited to lecture at other colleges on economic theory, she also gave talks on rowing and women's weightlifting. For those women who were just beginning to set foot on the water, they had little or no idea what they could or couldn't do.

Radcliffe women were often heckled on the Charles, and off the water, they were harassed by the press. Sports writers often focused on the foibles and the insecurities of women's rowing, instead of the excitement and the health rewards. A 1973 *Parade* article commented that "the principal complaint the girls come up with are calluses on their hands." One interviewee was even quoted as saying: "I can't touch my stockings without getting a run in them." A sports columnist from the *Boston Evening News* thought it was humorous to begin his coverage of a local woman's regatta with the lead: "Who says the female of the species is a lousy driver? They were all over the Charles River last Sunday and had only one collision."

Gail had dealt with reporters before, many of whom had mocked women's participation in rowing. Even *The New York Times* had given its spin to the growing interest in women's rowing, calling it the "Amazon syndrome," where women had taken up "weightlifting, ergometers, running the steps of the stadiums, and the flattening of the bosom." When they had asked Gail for a comment on this, she had kept her words tidy and direct, hammered into a slogan: *"It's all right to be strong. It's all right to compete."*

A lot of the negative attitude, she realized, was cultural. Guns and muscles belonged to men; they were manifestations of male power. But shooting or rowing, like many other sporting activities, were simply traditional ways that boys could develop essential strength and inner confidence that came with the mastery of a physical skill. Women needed access to that same source of confidence.

Her message, it seemed, had begun to take root. Over the past year, a number of young women had begun to appear in Boston, having heard the buzz that something exciting might happen on the Charles. Some, like Sue Morgan, Maggie MacLean, and Nancy

Storrs, showed up with nothing but a suitcase in hand and a burning desire to row. They had no jobs, no real career plans. Others were still in college but equally committed—like Wiki Royden, the Radcliffe rower. Instead of spending her summers back home in California, she stayed in Cambridge and learned how to scull.

Gail helped them in whatever way she could. She got Maggie and Nancy jobs at the Cambridge Boat Club, where they painted the locker rooms or helped haul boats in and out of the water. She loaned her single scull to Wiki, who turned out to be as gifted at sculling as she was in school (she'd entered Radcliffe at age sixteen). But as the crop of young women rowers gathered in Boston, it was a mixed blessing for Gail herself.

They wanted everything they could get from rowing—and they wanted it fast. Some of them were quite talented, like Wiki, and with their collegiate experience they quickly excelled at the sport that Gail had struggled long and hard to learn. In less than a year, they'd started rowing in fours and then eights, borrowing Radcliffe's rowing equipment, and even getting volunteer coaches. They called themselves the Eastern Development Camp, and invited Gail to row with them, even though she was a sculler and had never rowed sweep.

She chided some of the younger women like Nancy Storrs, who complained about not having everything they needed. Philosophically, Gail was certainly no Billie Jean King, who took an open, adversarial stance toward the male establishment. That, she felt, was counterproductive in the long run. Behind the scenes, Gail was waging her battles against the rowing establishment. But in public and on the surface, she always tried to focus on what was positive, to maintain the forward momentum. It was a hard concept for some of them, who felt they should have everything given to them all at once, and wanted to yell and scream to get it. Some things you fought for, and some you didn't. Hers was a strategic feminism, not a shotgun approach.

As in rowing itself, developing and expressing power was only one half of the equation for success. One portion of the stroke was known as the *drive*, where you used your force to lever the oars against the water and propel the boat forward. Women had to learn not to be afraid of developing and expressing that raw strength. But then there was the other equally important part of the stroke called the *recovery*, where the oars were out of the water getting ready for the next stroke. This required finesse, because if you weren't balanced or smooth, you would upset the forward momentum of the boat and subtract a lot of the power you'd just worked so hard to produce.

It took most rowers at least a few years to gain this control, to understand this concept of self-restraint between strokes. It was a subtle lesson in rowing that Gail applied to life. It had to do with poise on and off the water. And so, during NAAO meetings, when some of her male adversaries started yelling and screaming, she would never raise her voice or let her emotions get the best of her. Nor would she back off, her voice firm, almost unemotional, rational, persuasive, politic. Most of the time at least.

But the other lesson, the one that she had to face up to herself, was that the group effort had far greater impact than the individual effort. She'd won the Head of the Charles Regatta six years in a row now, but it was getting harder and harder to hold off the younger challengers. She was thirty-four, at the peak of her rowing powers, but soon she'd be losing the cardiovascular ability to maintain speed for the intense sprints. It was hard to be a single sculler, to hold that mental and physical edge year after year.

The previous fall, in her single, Radcliffe's Wiki Royden had placed second to Gail in the Head of the Charles—finishing only twenty seconds behind. Gail had been able to hold off the younger sculler over the winding, three-mile course, which favored a veteran like herself who knew the turns well. But this spring, Wiki had already beaten her once in a sprint, a short, straight course where there was nowhere for Gail to use her endurance or steering prowess. Even Sy Cromwell had been impressed by Wiki's progress, and had asked her to row a mixed double with him. Clearly something had to be done. The two were slated to row against each other at the Nationals, less than two months away.

Slowly, Gail had begun to realize that she'd nearly reached her limit, both on and off the water. She had taken herself, and women's rowing, as far as she could. Now the fate of U.S. women's rowing lay in other people's hands, like the Women's Olympic Rowing Committee, the group she had founded, but which had recently made some decisions that didn't bode well for her rowing career. Still, it was awfully hard to give up rowing now, with the Olympic debut only a year away. How could she make it to Montreal?

One of the WORC decisions had been to keep the sculling effort located in Long Beach, California, rather than to transport it to the East Coast. Joan Lind, the 1973 finalist in the single, was training there, as well as a group of others Gail had sometimes rowed with in doubles and quads. It made perfect sense to leave them there, training with their coach Tom McGibbon, but when she heard the decision, Gail flew off the handle at Bernie Horton—a member of the committee and a friend at the Cambridge Boat Club who had made the Long Beach recommendation.

"You've just ruined my chances!" she shouted. There was no way that she could give up her teaching and move out West to train properly with the other scullers.

Nonplussed, Bernie suggested that she consider switching over to sweep rowing and try out for the eight. The sweep camp would take place right in Boston, if they could secure their first choice for the coach. Gail quickly dismissed this as an outrageous suggestion; she was still too angry with Bernie for betraying her. A few weeks later, however, she had a change of heart. If nothing else, she was a pragmatist.

Even if she did beat Wiki Royden at the Nationals, she realized that the small talent pool of American scullers would be hard-pressed to win against the talented Europeans. As a sculler, she realized she had done what she could do. She had made her mark, and it was time to move on—leave the single to someone else. She would certainly go to the Nationals to compete against Wiki, but meanwhile she started training with the group of younger women who had come to Boston to be part of the eight—the one that might go to the World Championships in Nottingham as part of the first National Team Camp.

THE NATIONALS that were being held in Princeton that June would also serve as the initial tryout site for the first U.S. Women's Rowing Camp—the first step toward building a successful Olympic team. Any interested oarswomen would stay on for a few days after the conclusion of the regatta and perform a series of tests. Those who made the first cut would be invited to Boston, where the appointed coach would make further selections. In the end, eight rowers, a coxswain, and two spares would travel to Nottingham, England, and row at the World Championships. Few outside the rowing community would take notice of this race, but it was an important prelude to the women's rowing debut in the 1976 Olympics. The American public did follow that event, and the way things were going, the U.S. women would fare poorly.

Prior to this year, the winning crew of the Women's Nationals would have simply gone on intact to compete at the World Championships—the international race held during non-Olympic years. It was the same antiquated system of choosing a U.S. crew that had existed for years. Up until the 1960s, in fact, it had worked well for the U.S. men's eights teams, both at the Worlds and the Olympics. Represented by an eight-man crew from either Navy, the University of California, or Yale, the U.S. men hadn't lost the Olympics since 1920. Then Germany won in 1960, the last year an intact college crew was sent overseas to do battle with the Europeans. Something different had to be done. In 1964, a club crew of college grads from Vesper Boat Club in Philadelphia took back the gold, but soon after that, when the medals became more difficult to come by, the men had begun to consider a camp selection process.

The women were still following the old system, and it wasn't working. First-place honors at the Nationals often went to the Philadelphia clubs, composed of college grads who had a little more time together in a boat than the various fledgling undergraduate programs. The Philadelphia Girls Rowing Club and Vesper Boat Club were two of these. Still, when a club like Vesper went overseas to compete against the Europeans, they never finished better than seventh place. The new camp system, created by the Women's Olympic Rowing Committee, sought to select the best college and club rowers and form a kind of all-star crew that might fare better against their European rivals.

Despite her love for sculling, the idea of an eight appealed to Gail. It was the boat most people thought of when they thought about crew. And, from a practical standpoint, it was easier to get an eight moving fast in short order, requiring far less individual skill than in sculling. Besides, there were lots more sweep rowers than scullers. In the previous fall's Head of the Charles Regatta, there had been forty-two women's eights alone—a mere five years after her first solo appearance. An eight that harvested the young talent from all the new collegiate rowing programs would be an exciting boat indeed. If she couldn't beat the younger rowers, perhaps it was time to join forces with them.

There were a few obstacles in her path. First, she'd have to switch over to sweep rowing, to learn how to manipulate a large single oar instead of two. She wasn't too worried about that; most scullers found it easy to switch to sweep, and had a better sense of how to move a boat from rowing a single.

But was she too old at thirty-four?

At the camp she'd be competing for a seat against women at least ten years younger, who might not be any stronger but who could recuperate from hard workouts much faster. Well, she couldn't do anything about that; she'd have to rely on her superior race experience and time on the water. Over the years, she had developed the body of an oarswoman by putting in hundreds of miles on the river in her single. She'd also supplemented it with four years of weight training. Surely that was worth something and would give her an edge over the younger women. But now it took longer to recuperate, the soreness staying in her muscles through the next day.

Often, after she'd done her standard workout upstream, she paddled downstream another half mile to cool off and help her body flush out the lactic acid that had accumulated in her arms and legs. Just below the Cambridge Boat Club lay Newell, the Harvard men's boathouse. In the afternoon, the sun shone brilliantly upon the castle-like structure, with its wine-red slate shingles and four corner towers. The *Sports Illustrated* reporter who had recently come to write about Gail had been quite taken with it, and described it in passing as "the summer pavilion of some mad king." It was certainly the bastion of men's rowing in Boston, and behind its doors lay another key to Gail's success—an unusual man named Harry Parker.

In addition to her personal challenges, the most important thing to make the new camp work was to find a good coach, someone who could not only select the right crew and train them up to international standards, but a person who could lead a team of U.S. women to victory. Parker, she thought, would be perfect. He had more rowing knowledge than anyone she knew, and an inner quality that Gail had seen in other men who really knew how to get things done. When Parker spoke, everyone listened. Besides, with someone like him on their side, the women would have a powerful ally and wouldn't have to deal with some of the more troublesome political matters that had plagued them in the past.

She'd had some dealings with him before, as a fellow rowing enthusiast and as a former colleague at Harvard College. One time, while she was still teaching at the university, he'd even tracked her down on the river in his distinctive red launch when she was urgently needed on campus to help quell a student demonstration. And when her women's quadrascull had gone to Germany in 1972, Parker had been overseas with his Harvard men and had helped them procure a decent boat.

A few months earlier, when she had finally taken Bernie Horton's suggestion to go over to sweep and try out for the National Team, Parker had agreed to help her make the switch. He'd taken her into the indoor rowing tanks that were normally reserved for his Harvard men, and as he began to coach her, Gail realized how good he was not only in terms of his rowing knowledge, but the economical way he conveyed it. It was then that she decided that he was the best one for the job.

Behind closed doors at the Harvard athletic department, her friend Bernie Horton had also nominated Parker. It was during another WORC meeting, and a heated discussion had arisen over the right choice for the women's crew coaching position. It had been hard enough to even agree on the camp; now several arguments had broken out on this new concern, with each board member lobbying for their favorite person. Horton, a former coxswain, whose sonorous voice could still instantly gather attention, finally suggested that the accomplishments of each candidate be listed on a piece of paper, beside his name. That way, the merits of each could be surveyed.

After this was done, the room fell oddly silent. No one could dispute Parker's superiority, especially his international experience.

But would he do it? Would he take on a group of women?

F i v e

~~~

I N A W A Y, Harry Parker was an unlikely candidate for the job
of coaching the first women's team camp. True, he had
amassed an impressive record of wins during his twelve-year
tenure as head coach of the Harvard Crew, turning the varsity
heavyweight program into a virtually unstoppable juggernaut.
Since he'd taken the helm in 1962, Harvard hadn't lost a single
Harvard–Yale duel, beginning the longest dry spell for Yale in the
100-year history of the country's oldest intercollegiate sporting
event. Parker's current varsity eight and its predecessor, the infamous "Rude and Smooth Crew," had won back-to-back National
Championships, not losing a single race along the way.

At the relatively young age of thirty-nine, Parker was already
regarded as one of the most innovative and successful coaches in
recent rowing history—one whose reputation and influence
extended well beyond the realm of college crew. Like other famous
coaches—Bill Bowerman in track, John Wooden in basketball,
Vince Lombardi in football—his name had become part of the
public domain, had come to represent something about the sport
itself. *Sports Illustrated* had even run a cover story on him. Now,

when people talked about rowing, they talked about Harvard Crew; when they talked about Harvard Crew, they talked about Harry Parker.

There was no doubt in Gail Pierson's mind that Harry was the best person for the job. But why would a man like this want to coach a motley crew of women?

Only five years previously, in fact, Parker had been approached by a group of Radcliffe undergraduates wanting to start a women's rowing program. He had personally discouraged the idea, and it took the help of a few of his Harvard oarsmen to get the fledgling program off the ground. Even after the Radcliffe varsity eight won the National Championships in 1973 and went on to represent the U.S. in the World Championships in Moscow, Parker was still not sure what he thought about women's rowing. Sure, there might be a few individuals willing to work hard enough to move a boat well, but a real crew in his eyes still meant a crew of men.

Still, there were reasons why he might take the women on board. Just a few months earlier, he had been passed over for the U.S. Men's National Team coaching post, which was given instead to Al Rosenberg. Parker had originally held the post in 1972, when the camp system was first put in place. As the winningest coach in America, whose varsity had represented the U.S. in the '68 Olympic Games, he was the obvious choice for the job. Then Steve Gladstone, his lightweight coach, had taken the post for a year. Rosenberg, a former coxswain from Vesper Boat Club, had been next. While the men's camp system was still in its nascency, an effort was made to rotate the coach every year, to give different men a chance to make it work. The rotation was also in place because the position offered very little pay, and one person couldn't be expected to carry on such volunteer work over a long period of time.

Unsurprisingly, the U.S. camp teams performed with varying degrees of success, but the overall feeling was that the new "all-star" system worked. Parker's boat won a silver in the Olympics in

Munich, but Gladstone's crew was only sixth in Moscow at the 1973 Worlds. Then Al Rosenberg had taken the U.S. team to Lucerne in 1974 and had come back with a gold. For this performance, he was being given the team again.

Parker cited Rosenberg's recent success when reporters asked him about being passed up for the U.S. men's coaching job, but he was clearly disappointed with the decision. Harry had known Al Rosenberg for years, not only because the crew world was a small one, but because they had both emerged from the dynamic Philadelphia rowing scene of the 1950s, and they had both been members of Vesper Boat Club. And yet they were very different men, with very different approaches to coaching crew.

Ten years earlier in 1964, soon after Parker had taken over the helm of the Harvard varsity, Rosenberg had begun his leadership of the Vesper squad. Both men had produced the fastest crews in the country that year, and as it was the pre-camp era, the two eights rowed against each other to decide which one would represent the U.S. at the Olympics. It was a classic confrontation, the finest club crew going up against the finest college boat, and Vesper won by a narrow margin. Under Rosenberg's command, Vesper went on to prove their worth, rowing to gold at the Tokyo Games.

Parker had not forgotten the loss—the only blemish in his first undefeated season.

His recent undefeated seasons, '74 and '75, had been reminiscent of that previous decade, when he had made his coaching debut. After a shaky start as a first-year freshman coach, he was thrust prematurely into the varsity post when his boss, Harvey Love, died suddenly of a heart attack. Many expected the young coach to fail—he was only twenty-six, and his first-year record with the freshman team was a dismal 1–3. He'd never even coached crew before he'd come to Harvard, and he had come to be there largely by happenstance.

Parker did have a decent rowing pedigree. He'd rowed on the Penn varsity, under the tutelage of the legendary Philadelphia sculler Joe Burk, who was seen as one of the luminaries in the sport. Under Burk, Parker had learned a lot about rowing and certainly knew what it meant to win. A mere 174 pounds, Parker had made the Penn varsity boat three years in a row, winning the Eastern Sprints and the Royal Henley Regatta. After that, however, he'd joined the Navy, and might have never held an oar again if he hadn't come across an unaddressed circular to all members of the armed services. The circular outlined procedures for those who wished to row for their country in the 1959 Pan-Am Games, and the Rome Olympics the following year.

Parker immediately wrote to Burk, asking him if he thought he'd make a decent sculler. When Burk replied in the affirmative and agreed to take him on as a protégé, Parker quickly requested a transfer to Philadelphia where he could train as a national team oarsman. As his old coach predicted, he did quite well in the single, winning the 1959 American Championships and a gold medal at the Pan-Am Games. The next year he was selected as the U.S. single sculler for the 1960 Olympics in Rome, and finished a respectable fifth in a field of talented Europeans.

Parker had never really intended to be a single sculler, which took a lot of skill and years of practice. He imagined he might row in a double or a four. Most of the great single scullers began their careers early on; Parker had only trained for a few years. His sculling technique wasn't particularly graceful; his quick progress was due mainly to hard work and a competitive zeal that Burk had identified early on. Others noticed it too. (Jim Barker, a fellow Philadelphia sculler, thought that pound for pound there was no one that pushed himself harder or conducted himself in a more sportsmanlike manner than Parker.) While Parker was competing at Henley in '59 in the Diamond Sculls, Harvey Love had been so impressed after talking with Parker about rowing, that he recommended the young man for the freshman coaching job when it became available the following year.

Parker fell into the job more as a matter of fate than as something planned or even self-executed. Despite his obvious enthusiasm for rowing, he'd never imagined himself as a coach. This attitude was typical of most American crew coaches, who got into a launch thinking that it might be a fun way to spend a few years while figuring out what to do with their lives. In the U.S., there was very little money for rowing coaches, and even less social status. In some of the Eastern Bloc countries like East Germany, crew coaches actually studied for the job and served a lengthy apprenticeship under a veteran coach.

When Love died unexpectedly in the middle of Parker's third year, his apprenticeship was brought to an abrupt end. For the remainder of the term, he was asked to take over as the head coach of Harvard Crew, a much larger responsibility than he was qualified for, or so many people thought. It was one thing to be a freshman coach, after all, and quite another to run an entire program and coach the varsity squad, which carried the hopes and dreams of countless Harvard alums who expected nothing more than total success. More than a few imagined that the young coach would simply serve as a short-term stand-in, until a better replacement for Love could be found the next fall. Instead, Parker took the '63 varsity through a 3–1 season, capped with an impressive victory over Yale.

Harry Parker was at Harvard to stay.

Formally installed as the new head coach, Parker's crews began to surpass all expectations, to get better and better every season. In 1964, the varsity went 4–0, winning the Eastern Sprints Championship. The next year the crew not only went undefeated, but also rowed virtually unchallenged by other crews and smashed numerous records along the way. Over the standard spring racing distance of 2000 meters, the closest crew was two-and-a-half boat lengths behind—virtual light-years in rowing terms. At the annual Harvard–Yale Race held in New London every June, Harvard beat its Ivy League rival by an embarrassing ten boat lengths at the end of the four-mile course—one of the largest margins ever.

These remarkable feats amazed everyone in the crew world, and even led those beyond it to speculate about the winning nature of this coach and his crimson crew. Some said it was the equipment—the special boat Parker had shipped over from Switzerland—and the unorthodox way he had rigged it, adopting a "German" configuration with two starboard seats back to back. Parker had bought new British oars as well, with shorter shafts and wider blades.

Others, like rival coach Dutch Schoch of Princeton, were convinced that Harvard's speed had more to do with the new way of rowing Parker had introduced and the method of training that accompanied it. The orthodox American style at the time involved a studied, slow approach to each "catch" (where the blades entered the water), which allowed the boat a long, extended glide when the oars were out of the water (during the recovery portion of the stroke cycle). Visually, the technique looked long and graceful, like a large bird beating its wings and still making good speed.

Parker's technique, developed from the Germans, involved a shorter, quicker motion with no wasted time, or pause, up at the catch. Instead of slowing down as they came forward to the beginning of each stroke, the Harvard oarsmen would literally dive for the catch, unleashing all their power upon first contact with the water. The overall effect was a more compact, "punchier" stroke that often pushed the Harvard crew along at a slightly higher stroke rate than most of its competitors.

But beyond the special boat and oars, the seating arrangement, the new rowing technique, and the training methods, there was something unmistakably special about Parker himself, a quiet, often brooding man. Successful coaches had more than just a knowledge about their sport; they had charisma, a personal confidence that could be transferred to the members of the team. Usually this kind of power came with time, after a coach had won again and again and he was older and wiser. But Parker had earned this respect early on, while he was still a relatively young coach.

He was a different kind of coach than most sports fans were used to, as different as the sport he coached. Behind the studied, silent air was an intelligent, piercing look that the press, for lack of a better word, called patrician. His coaching style was minimalist. He had no need to yell to get people to do what he wished. Likewise, he was reluctant to take credit from or give credit to his crews, and to make generalizations about life or rowing. This close-mouthed style left those around him to marvel and speculate about the secret of his success. The press seemed to love him for it—and sensed a legend in the making.

The *Sports Illustrated* cover had all the glamorous elements of a good cigarette ad. It displayed the young Parker in the foreground, with his chiseled good looks, looking out confidently from the page with his muscular forearms crossed casually in front of him. His bright crimson shirt matched the color of his Harvard crew, rowing by in the background through a field of sea-green water.

It was flattering to a fault, including the optimistic caption, which read: HARVARD COACH HARRY PARKER AND THE WORLD'S BEST CREW.

Parker, it turned out, didn't have the best crew in the world. That honor belonged to the Vesper eight, and to the diminutive ex-coxswain Allen Perry Rosenberg. It was Rosenberg who had given Parker and his '64 Harvard crew the only blemish to their perfect record. Now, ten years later, Rosenberg was back, after disappearing for a while to pursue a more lucrative career as a lawyer. Unlike Parker, he'd never been fortunate enough to be offered a full-time, Ivy League coaching post that could afford him the opportunity to stay in rowing and support a family.

Despite this, he had taken the U.S. men's team post away from Parker—this time by assignment and not even by force.

Parker's predicament was the women's gain. With Rosenberg's

return as the coach of the U.S. men's eight, the Women's Olympic Rowing Committee had seen their chance to nab one of the premier coaches in the country. But when they first put the proposal to him that winter, Parker had initially balked and said he'd have to think about it. The women's national team coaching job was, after all, a position that carried absolutely no status. Among Parker's colleagues, women's rowing was little more than a curious new phenomenon that was somehow moving forward, against the strong current of cultural resistance.

In the end, despite his doubts, he decided to take the job. He would start working with some of the local candidates that spring, the EDC group that included Gail Pierson and Wiki Royden, but he couldn't turn his full attention to the official summer camp until mid-July, after he finished his 1975 spring season. His Harvard varsity was on the rise again, the finest squad in years. Another undefeated season and a recent victory over Yale meant a trip to Henley would be in order. There, they would race against all comers— including Rosenberg's U.S. team, the so-called world champions.

Now plans for the women's camp had only one more hitch, and its name was Vesper.

S i x

VESPER BOAT CLUB was a stronghold of club rowing, one of the old Philadelphia clubs that lined the Schuylkill River and made up the alliance known as the Schuylkill Navy. Vesper was where Al Rosenberg had learned his trade, along with a distinguished membership of oarsmen that had probably won more medals than any other club in America. They had complained about the new camp idea for women, arguing that a group of diverse individuals who would spend eight weeks together were no match for a set crew that had worked together for several seasons. They had even contested the camp system in court and won a temporary injunction that allowed them to challenge the new selection process—*if* they won the 1975 Women's Nationals in May.

Based on past history, Vesper was confident that they could do this. The only serious challenge would be from the newly founded group of Boston oarswomen who called themselves the Eastern Development Camp, coached by ex-Princeton oar Peter Raymond, and now being shepherded by Harry Parker. The only college team that might pose an outside threat was Radcliffe, which had upset them two years earlier. Radcliffe had just won the Eastern Sprints again, the big collegiate race held in May, narrowly beating a group of upstarts from the University of Wisconsin.

The inside story at the Eastern Sprints, however, was that Radcliffe had coasted through an easy heat in the morning, rowing virtually unchallenged. In the other heat, Wisconsin had battled fiercely with Yale and Princeton to make it through to the final. Part of the problem for Wisco was that they were getting used to a new racing shell, which had just been delivered, unrigged, to the race site in Middletown, Connecticut. To change boats just before a race was to invite disaster—especially a rounder, tippier one like the Schoenbrod they had ordered.

Boatbuilder Helmut Schoenbrod made a different boat than the Seattle-built shells of English expatriate George Pocock. The Pocock shells were made from traditional wooden materials, had relatively flat hulls, and "fixed" riggers. They were a no-fuss, easy-to-balance boat. For years, Pocock, whose advertising slogan was "Building Boats to Help Build Manhood," had served American crews well. But Schoenbrod had different ideas. His hull was to be the first successful American boat made out of glass fiber, making it a little lighter than the wood counterpart but just as strong. It had a rounder bottom, too, which would yield more speed for a technically adept crew, and the riggers could be adjusted to achieve the right amount of "load" the crew had to bear on each stroke.

The lighter hull and adjustable riggers would prove a boon to women's crews, which had generally been handling oversized hand-me-downs from men's crews. Unfortunately, Wisconsin coach Jay Mimier didn't have the first idea about how to rig the newfangled fiberglass boat. With the old Pococks, all he had to do was bolt the metal riggers on the wooden hull, an operation similar in ease to taking the wheels on and off a bicycle. The fully adjustable riggers of the new boat were a mystery to him—what were the proper dimensions for a women's crew? Finally, he asked the Yale women's coach, Nat Case, if he could run a tape measure over his

Schoenbrod, an identical boat, and copy the various settings of the oarlocks. Graciously, the Yale coach agreed.

What Case couldn't provide was the time necessary for the rowers to adjust to the lighter, tippier boat. The Wisconsin crew was a young crew, and not so technically adept that they could make such a major adjustment with ease. They slogged through their heat, wasting a lot of energy to hold off Princeton and Yale. For the afternoon final, they were too tired to take on Radcliffe, a crew they might have handled easily in their old boat.

While Carie Graves and the varsity were struggling with their new boat and their East Coast rivals, the Wisco freshmen won their race easily by two lengths of open water—an enormous margin that got Mimier thinking. After the race, he decided to take three of these freshmen rowers—Peggy MacCarthy, Mary Grace Knight, and Jackie Zoch—and promote them into the varsity eight. Equipment issues aside, the varsity should not have lost to Radcliffe. Perhaps the three novices could lend some speed to the boat.

Back on Lake Mendota, his stopwatch confirmed his suspicions. The new varsity boat was starting to register impressive times—about three-and-a-half minutes for a 1000-meter piece. A week or so before the Nationals, he called the Princeton coach, Al Piranen, to finalize arrangements for their trip to New Jersey. While they were talking, the other coach grumbled about Vesper's court injunction. Piranen, whose crew had placed third at the Easterns, seemed resigned to the fact that the Philadelphia club would row away with the race and derail the U.S. camp selection process. Mimier was curious. How fast was Vesper? he asked. Piranen listed some 1000-meter times that were a few seconds slower than what Mimier's revamped varsity was doing. It was, of course, impossible to compare times taken on different bodies of water. It was hard enough to do this on the same stretch of water, due to the effects of shifting winds and currents.

Vesper rowed on the Schuylkill, a river with a measurable

amount of current to it. Wisconsin rowed on a large, unprotected lake. Still, Mimier wasn't overly impressed with the times Piranen listed. No, Vesper would have to do better than that, he glibly informed Piranen, or they would lose to his varsity squad. There was a brief pause at the other end of the line. Was Mimier simply cocky, or could his crew really go that fast?

To Carie Graves, the Princeton boathouse was an impressive sight—especially compared to the concrete bunker where Wisco rowed back in Madison. Its seven pointed-arch bay doors, opening out onto Lake Carnegie, had the look of cloisters. The stucco walls, corner tower, and structural buttresses added to the neo-Gothic look that characterized much of the architecture on the Princeton campus. It even had a huge ballroom on the second floor, with a fireplace and a cathedral ceiling. The more critical eye of an art historian might have concluded that the building was a somewhat dubious effort to mimic the style of Oxford and Cambridge. To Carie and her teammates, however, it was indeed grand.

Other parts of Princeton were equally impressive. After an easy workout on Thursday before the semi-final heats, Carie and four-seat Sue Ela were back at the Princeton dorms, washing up in the bathroom. On a dare, no doubt, a Princeton male undergraduate casually strode in, disrobed, and began to take a shower. The shower room was a big open stall with several nozzles, and Carie stood naked under one of them. The Princeton boy regarded her in silence, waiting to see how she would react. If he expected a scream, it never came. Having posed nude in front of an entire classroom, Carie was more curious than taken aback when she noticed the naked boy.

"Hi, how's it going?" she finally said to her mute shower mate, who quickly fetched his towel, dried off, and retreated. After he'd left, Carie called out to teammate Sue Ela: "Wow. These guys are *really* progressive around here. Even the showers are coed!"

In many ways, the Wisconsin women were a study in contrast to the Ivy League teams they'd come to compete against—as rough and ready as their team mascot. Rowing-wise, they plowed their way through the water with an imperfect sense of balance and finesse. In the eyes of a rowing purist, the Badgers were not a pretty sight. Part of their lack of polish was simply their inexperience. Part of it, as Jay Mimier put it, was that Wisconsin rowing, like their boathouse, had always been more utilitarian in nature.

Off the water, too, the women from Madison carried on in a more rustic fashion than their East Coast peers. If rowers were supposed to comport themselves with a subdued, serious air as they went about the business of unloading their boats, the Wisconsin women hadn't been properly schooled. They clowned around with each other, sang silly songs, and reputedly drank copious amounts of beer. (The team's theme song, in fact, had a chorus that ran: "If you can't drink beer like Wisco, go to hell!") Win or lose, Jay Mimier had brought along a case of Pabst Blue Ribbon to Princeton, stashed in the back of the truck that pulled the shell trailer.

Other teams had training rules and a dry-land code of conduct. Even though competitive women's rowing was a relatively new endeavor, it had taken some of its cues from the men's rowing that had preceded it, among them an unspoken sense of social propriety. Part of this Ivy League ethic was being passed along directly by the male coaches who were now teaching these young women to row. But Wisconsin had never really been a part of this sophisticated Ivy League mentality.

And if his team carried on like a bunch of sailors on shore leave, Mimier didn't seem to mind. He was a serious coach with a sense of humor. In the fall, he often joined his crew for the Friday night pitchers of beer that sold for fifty cents in the dorms. He liked the quirky sense of camaraderie that had developed within his young team, produced both by the Midwestern culture and the shared effort needed to bring the unlikely program into being. If this outlook drew disapproving stares and sarcastic grins from other crews, that was all right by him. In the back of his mind, he knew that his team needed their own sense of identity to use against the eastern crews, just as much as they needed to row their own race in the manner they chose.

Winning races was partly a matter of confidence, and Mimier knew it. Given crews that could row roughly the same speed, the team that believed they could win would generally hang together through the pain and prevail. In a seasoned program like Vesper, much of this confidence came through a lineage of victories, of numerous races where they had come out on top. They had the trophies to prove it, and a nice boathouse—like Princeton's—to put them in. Wisco barely raced anyone and didn't know exactly where they stood.

WISCONSIN'S SEMI-FINAL went off pretty much as expected on Friday, with Vesper first, the Eastern Development Camp second, and the Badgers third, but it had been close racing among the three qualifiers, which posted the fastest times of the day—3:30.7, 3:32, and 3:34.5. Yale, Princeton, and UCal Berkeley had qualified in the slower heat. Perhaps due to nerves, the Badgers had spent most of the race trying to recover from a clumsy start, rife with bad strokes. When they fell behind the leaders, Carie had increased the stroke rating to thirty-eight strokes per minute to try to make up the lost water. It was a kamikaze move, particularly into a headwind. A high cadence like that would generally kill a boat's "run"—the continuous, efficient glide forward between strokes. It also deprived a crew of oxygen, because a 38 was basically an all-out sprint.

Still, miraculously, they had qualified for the final. More important, they had only finished four seconds out of first, less than a boat length behind top-ranked Vesper. Radcliffe, which had beaten them at the Eastern Sprints, came in fourth and failed to qualify. Two things were readily apparent to everyone in the Wisconsin boat. First, they were definitely the best college crew. Second, Vesper and EDC were not invulnerable.

The next day, Jay Mimier, a man of few words before a race, gathered his Wisconsin squad under a giant beech tree. If nothing else, he would get them out of the unseasonable, eighty-degree heat. He spent a little time going over strategy with the crew, talking about getting a clean start and settling into a reasonable stroke rating. A six-boat race wasn't like a two-boat race. You couldn't just focus on beating one team, or another might slip by you unnoticed. Yet even as he said the words, he knew that little of this race talk would sink in right now. The race would go the way it would go, and there was not much he could say to them technically or strategy-wise that would help their performance at this point.

Mimier often looked uncomfortable when he tried to give these formal team speeches. He hooked his thumbs in the pockets of his jeans and stared down at the ground a lot—not a good start for someone who aspired to be a trial lawyer. Looking down as often as he did only called attention to his unkempt mane of brown hair and his size-fifteen purple high-top sneakers. Carie Graves thought he was the epitome of the Wisconsin farm boy—gangly, rawboned, and unpretentious. But here was the man that they had all come to love, who had been a large part of why she had stuck with crew.

He really didn't have much to say. Everything was either in place by now, or it wasn't. He'd put in the three freshman rowers and knew the boat was faster for it. Whether it was faster than EDC or Vesper, he couldn't say, and they couldn't waste time worrying about it. Worrying about the other crews just took away from your own focus and integrity. He looked at his athletes and knew that they were big and strong for a women's crew—the boat averaged about 5 feet 10 inches, 150 pounds. Perhaps they were a little intimidated by the Ivy League surroundings at Princeton. If that was the case, he had to get them to focus on themselves now, to remind them of what they were capable of doing.

While a sense of confidence and trust couldn't simply be handed down to a crew, they did look to him for some sense of their worth. His team had gone into the heat with no expectations, and had come out third to the two best crews in the country. If he wasn't sure that his women could beat Vesper, they would certainly sense his doubt and take it as a given limit to their ability. They were a young group of impressionable athletes who had no idea what they were capable of doing. For a group like this, psychology would play a big role in determining the race—bigger than anything else. And even if a coach couldn't secure a win, he could certainly endorse one.

He condensed these sentiments into a final send-off phrase:

"Go piss with the big dogs," he told them.

The comment had just the right amount of irreverence, humor, and challenge in it to put everyone at ease. Just after the speech, Carie's brother, Ross, her boyfriend Ira, and another member of the Wisconsin men's crew suddenly appeared, wearing ridiculous-looking rented tuxedos. They had driven non-stop from Madison to serve as the women's official cheering section. Mimier's speech and the sudden appearance of the men had restored a sense of Wisco integrity—much more than that, at least in Carie's mind. Princeton and the Ivies could have their fancy boathouses, she thought, we'll show them who really knows how to row.

Whatever naïveté or lack of seriousness Wisconsin may have presented on the outside, when it came down to racing they were transformed. Carie felt it in herself and saw it in her teammates. Shortly before launch time, an odd calmness fell over them. Their movements became automatic, almost ritualistic. They had gone over the boat to check for loose fittings. Their seats had been cleaned, oiled, and slid back into place. A malfunctioning seat that got stuck, or worse—popped off the tracks—could cost the crew a race.

If she had chosen to think about it this way, her fellow teammates acted a lot like soldiers preparing for war. Once the coxswain, Beth, had given the command to "lay hold," the entire crew fell into an intense, mindful silence. As they took hold of the boat, listening for the next command, it was as if they were taking hold of themselves—establishing a connection of total trust in one another. In this sense, in crew there was little need for any rah-rah pre-race meeting or joining of hands followed by a unified team shout. Done well, the simple but precise sequence—of bringing the boat to the water, affixing the oars to the boat, and getting seated and "tied in"—was all that was needed.

"*Hands on. Over the heads—ready, up.*" The shell was lifted overhead and briefly held aloft.

"*To the shoulders—ready, down.*" The rowers moved opposite their riggers and slowly lowered the boat down—ports resting the starboard gunwale on their shoulders, starboards resting the port gunwale on theirs.

Each movement, carried out in its proper sequence, helped displace that wrenching, individual uncertainty, and slowly filled the void with a sense of group solidarity. To Carie it imparted an almost electric feeling, which coursed through her limbs and made her feel almost invincible.

"*Walk it forward.*" This was it, they were heading toward the water. There was no turning back now.

"*Over the heads—ready, up.*" The narrow dock shifted a little under their feet. They bore the shell aloft again and reached inside for a solid handhold.

How light the boat felt now—as if it were not a boat, but merely a conduit that could take the puny efforts of eight individuals and somehow amplify them into a much greater force. This is what could happen in a good team like Wisco, and it was the secret ingredient of any top-notch crew. More than equipment or strategy or anything else, it was the essence of rowing power—the trust in the One. If you didn't have that, the rest hardly mattered. All you would have was a boat full of eight individuals, wrestling each other down the racecourse.

"*Roll it—ready, down.*" They placed the boat in the water, being careful not to knock out the delicate fin that helped the boat go straight. They fetched the wooden oars and fit them into their oarlocks, clamped down the gates and screwed them down tight. A loose gate could cost a crew a race, if the oar were to pop out of it.

"*Ports. Ship out your oars. One foot and down. Starboards, one foot and down. Tie in. Check your foot stretchers. Count down from bow when ready!*"

Each rower's voice sounded off for the last time, not as a name now but just a number or a seat position:

"*Bow. Two. Three. Four. Five. Six. Seven. Stroke.*"

And if crew could seem mechanical or even militaristic in one sense, it could also be very Zen-like in another. After all, there would be no real battle, no clashing of swords. The members of the crew weren't going to mix it up with another team, to smash their oars against one another and effect daring, heroic maneuvers. Instead, they were going to perform exactly the same motion together about a hundred times (about 100 strokes for a 1000-meter effort). If you wanted to carry the battle image forward, then rowers weren't a group of soldiers, but the weapon itself.

The Wisco crew shoved off and paddled away in silence. They were on their own now, with no one to tell them what to do.

A CREW COACH is utterly useless during a crew race, unable to communicate with his crew. Even if it were possible to talk to them as they raced, it was not permitted. Unlike coaches of other team sports, who could direct or at the very least assist their teams to victory, crew coaches had to remain silent during a regatta. On the one hand, it was nerve-wracking. On the other hand, it made perfect sense. If you shouted at your crew, it would take away from their concentration. Most coaches just stood at the finish line of a big race and waited nervously for their crew to arrive. Some got on bicycles and tried to follow the race from shore, hoping not to hit a tree or a spectator. If they were lucky or important, they might get to ride in the launch. Mimier stood on the shore.

For Friday's heat, he had stationed someone every 250 meters along the 1000-meter course, so that he could "see" his boat progress through each quarter of the race. He himself had stood at the 250-meter mark. In a way, a crew race was a play divided up into four acts—the start, the settle, the middle, and the sprint. These were all critical points where a crew could effect some degree of strategy. Ideally, his crew would get off to a clean start, with a flurry of quick, short strokes—precisely placed, so there would be no missed water at the catch or "crabs" at the finish. (Crabbing was when someone's blade got stuck underwater at the end of the stroke, either because the timing or position of the blade was off.) Small crabs would be disruptive to the motion of the crew, while larger ones could stop the boat from moving or actually throw a rower out of the boat.

After the initial acceleration off the line, the crew would "settle" or reduce its stroke rating to a more reasonable cadence. On the coxswain's command, the crew "shifted gears," slowing down into a more relaxed rhythm that could be sustained through the middle of the race. The settle wasn't a lessening of power on the stroke itself, just a slowing of the sliding seats in between strokes the gathering movement of the eight bodies as they prepared for the next catch. With good ratio, a crew could be at maximum speed and still look like they were barely working at all, there was so little rush or worry to their movement.

If a crew came off the line at forty strokes per minute, for example, they might settle somewhere between a 33 and a 36. After that, they might take "power tens" to try to move on a nearby opponent—a common strategy during the middle of a close race. When you were near an opponent, the idea was to "break" the other crew—to row through them and then hold off any countermove. If they took a ten, you countered with a ten, trying to maintain the lead. Once you were out of their visual range, it was a lot harder for them to move back *through* or even *to* you. Their coxswain could indicate your position to the backward-facing rowers, but that somehow didn't provide the same incentive as the real thing—besides, coxswains were notorious for providing optimistic estimates. No, having another boat right beside you was much better for motivation. Better yet, to have them right behind.

Finally, for the last twenty strokes of the race, there was the sprint. Once again, the stroke rating was raised, the relaxed ratio abandoned, in favor of a short, unsustainable burst of speed. If you had paced yourself well for the body of the race, you could sometimes catch up to a crew that had over-extended themselves in the early going.

This had been Wisco's plan in the heat, but it had all gone to hell with the bad start—and then Carie had never settled down, never allowed the crew to find a sense of steady rhythm. A much simpler way to row a crew race, of course, was to go off the line at full tilt, get ahead of the other boats and just not let them pass you. To a young crew, which lacked the patience or confidence to pace their efforts, this strategy made a lot more sense. To Carie, it was the only way to row—pacing your power was a cop-out, was just another form of comparing yourself to other boats to gauge your effort.

By the time the open eights final rolled around, the wind had shifted from a head wind to a tail wind. That was good news, Mimier thought, if Carie tried to jack the stroke rating up again. He had cautioned her not to, but she had a mind of her own. This time, he stationed himself right at the finish line. Whatever came before it hardly mattered anymore.

Back in the boat at the starting line, Carie Graves was thinking none of these thoughts. Not the boat, not technique, not the boy in the shower. Not her father and his theory about the rewards of crew all coming through self-sacrifice. Not even Vesper, sitting ready in the lane beside them. All these thoughts were just distractions to the real challenge at hand—the battle that would take place inside her mind.

She hadn't talked about this much or told any of her teammates—how during a race she entered a different state of mind, one where pure aggression ruled and pain was personified as an enemy force. A few times during particularly hard workouts, she had allowed herself to explore the depths of her subconscious mind, penetrating the pain barrier to where the demons lay. Sometimes an evil being like the devil appeared and asked her if she would sell her soul for excellence—all she had to do was take the power down, to back off from an all-out effort.

"No," she would reply, "I won't do it."

Fortunately, standing at the finish line, Mimier didn't witness any of this. Nor did he see the way Carie came off the line at full tilt, never really settling into a rational race pace. When the other crews settled, she just kept sprinting—exactly what he had cautioned against. What he did see was a rough-looking but very determined Badger boat, barreling down the racecourse at thirty-nine strokes a minute, ahead of all the other crews. Carie was stroking three or four beats higher than the rest of the field, pulling another kamikaze maneuver. In the tail wind, however, she was getting away with it—if the rest of the crew could stay with her. Vesper was closing now for the sprint, closing the gap with every stroke they took. As the crews crossed the finish line, Wisconsin fell apart, the port side crabbing their oars in the water.

The boat came to a sudden, ungraceful stop—but they had beaten Vesper by 3.3 seconds.

As they paddled back to receive their gold medals, the crew quickly fell back into their clownish behavior. The coxswain, Beth Traut, switched places with Sue Ela—a move that made the boat look more ungainly than ever. No one, at this point, seemed to care. Scattered images of sweet reality danced in Carie's mind. A group of strange men in suit coats, hugging her on the dock. Jay Mimier, with a case of Pabst Blue Ribbon. Beth, the coxswain, being thrown into the water. Her mind was adrift now, completely unfocused, flooded with an excess of oxygen and emotion.

The suit coats were Olympic Committee officials who had come to the regatta and nervously watched the race, secretly rooting for Wisconsin. By defeating Vesper, the Badgers had saved the whole selection camp—and provided every woman there with a chance to make the U.S. team. Theoretically, if they had wanted to, Wisconsin could have seized the victor's right to row at the Worlds—something no Wisconsin team had ever done. Humbly, they declined. Most of the women in the boat had done better than they had ever dreamed possible.

For Carie, however, the dream had just begun. It had unfolded almost according to plan. Months before, when she had spoken to a women's group in Madison, trying to raise money, she had boldly told them they would win the Nationals. Now that it had actually happened, it felt unreal. It was as if, in rowing, she could control her own fate. Perhaps that was the mysterious reward her father had alluded to, the payoff for all that hard work and pain.

The Wisconsin women didn't get any betting shirts that day— the standard custom among men's teams. Soon, however, Carie and her teammates, Jackie Zoch and Sue Ela, would be trying to trade in their Wisconsin shirts for a sleeveless U.S.A. shirt of nearly the same shade of red.

They were heading to Boston.

HARRY'S
HOUSE

Seven

HARVARD UNIVERSITY was not only known as the best college in the country, it was one of the premier places to row. It had one of the finest facilities in the entire United States, if not the world. The main campus of the 150-year-old college was only a few blocks from the Charles River, and several of its Georgian brick residence halls lined the banks of the waterway. If they'd felt like it, Carie Graves and her roommate, Jackie Zoch, could have pitched a rock into the river from a third-floor window of the Eliot House dorm where they were staying.

A badly aimed throw would have hit Weld, one of Harvard's two elegant boathouses. Most American colleges were fortunate enough to have one boathouse, usually a converted barn or an out-building like the old Coast Guard station that became the first home of the University of Washington Crew. Both of Harvard's boathouses, built around the turn of the twentieth century, had been outfitted with an eye for architectural style as well as practical function.

Weld, originally built to encourage a broad-based university-wide interest in rowing, had an Edwardian look to it with brick-lined stucco walls. Its huge clay-tiled roof sheltered six long boat bays with elegant, vaulted ceilings that made the interior look like a giant wine cellar. Instead of wine, however, Weld had the capacity for over eighty boats—from single sculls to intramural eights. It was here that Wiki Royden had taken her first strokes, as a member of the Radcliffe Crew that had recently taken up residence there.

The women's camp, however, wasn't running out of Weld, but across the river at Newell, the men's boathouse. As the recruits walked over the Anderson Bridge during the first week of practice, they retraced the steps of countless Harvard freshmen rowers who wandered innocently across the river for the first time only to encounter something very different from anything they'd ever seen before. Newell was an elegant but odd-looking Victorian castle, standing alone on the far bank of the river. It was well situated away from the college campus and all the hustle and bustle of Harvard Square. Unlike the concrete and steel football stadium that stood behind it, Newell harkened back to an earlier time, where style and substance had found their balance.

Its most striking feature was its coat of red slate shingles. If there was any confusion in a new recruit's mind as to where he would find the Harvard Crew, the crimson exterior was a dead giveaway. Its greenish-gray slate roof was its only demure feature, and even this was elegantly trimmed and tasseled. Copper flashing ran down the ridge beams of its four corner towers, each of which had a cupola and a brass spire on top. The ornamentation of the roofs, together with the slightly upturned edges of its overhangs, gave Newell a grand, almost Asian look, like an elegant pagoda.

Because its bays had a northern exposure, it was a boathouse that showed best at the end of the day, as the falling light reflected off the water and gave the brick red shingles a golden, fiery glow. Just after sunset, lit up from within, it was brilliant when viewed from the Anderson Bridge or from the opposite bank—the yellow light streaming out of its bays and illuminating the dark waters of the Charles. With such a regal exterior, an outsider might speculate that wonderful parties took place behind its walls at night, spilling out onto docks and balconies.

In reality, however, one step inside revealed a stark, almost grim interior that most newcomers found quite intimidating. When you entered the doors of the Harvard Boathouse for the first time, it was as if you had stepped through the looking glass and into a house of giants. Everything about Newell was huge and forbidding.

Perhaps it was merely the proportions of the place, the physical hugeness that made a newcomer feel so small. As you entered the building on the bottom floor, you immediately walked into four seventy-foot-long bays with twenty-foot ceilings, dimensions called for by the extreme length of the boats and the oars. At rest, the sixty-foot-long shells were racked directly on top of one another, bunk-bed fashion, supported by several thick beams that stuck out from massive oaken posts like the branches of a tree. The twelve-and-a-half-foot oars stood up vertically in soldierly rows, their narrow, blood-red blade design making them look a little like medieval pikes.

Perhaps it was the northern orientation of the bays, which left the building dark and shadowy even during the day. Or the unique collection of strong, earthy smells—of sweat, river, and varnished wood. From the workshop, on the east side of the bays, came the smell of freshly sawn cedar or spruce; from the west side came the dank odor of the indoor rowing tanks, sitting in their moats of still water.

Perhaps it had something to do with the monastic silence that prevailed in the building when a coach or a coxswain wasn't directing a crew about. Whatever it was, Newell had a way of challenging anyone who stepped through its doors, regardless of their prior background. It was both haunting and enchanting, but never a place where you'd want to be alone at night.

Despite the odd silence, Newell had more than a sense of history to it. There was a living, breathing presence made up of all those who had come through its doors and added their sweat and muscle to nearly a century of Harvard crews gone by. At the top of the six-foot-wide staircase, there was a large open room that was filled with a battery of metal ergometers and specialized weight equipment that Parker had brought in for the purpose of strengthening arms, backs, and legs. Banners from old races were slung from the trussed beams of the high ceilings, and along the walls were other displays of Harvard victories from the past 100 years, ribbons and cups and old black-and-white photos of the serious-looking men who had won them—standing with their arms crossed, faces full of silent expectation.

For all its starkness, Newell had a rough elegance to it that one might expect in an Anglo Saxon hall. It was partly like Harry Parker himself: understated, utilitarian, but strong and confident. Some thought that Newell's ambiance was partly a reflection of Harry's personality. Others thought that the elegant but austere building had in fact shaped him—that Parker, too, had felt the pressure at Harvard when he arrived, and had risen to the challenge. Now he expected everyone else to do the same.

Several of the thirty-two women trying out for the team had heard stories about Harry from their own coaches; others had actually worked with him a little already. Carie's coach, Jay Mimier, had rowed under Parker. So had Wiki Royden's Radcliffe coach, John Baker. Everyone, it seemed, had a story to tell about him, and it usually had to do with some strange, unpredictable behavior that somehow, in the end, yielded a favorable result.

For his new undergraduate men, at least, Parker wore an expression that didn't invite intimacy. One former oarsman described it as a studied look of perpetual dissatisfaction, an unsettling mask that kept young Harvard overachievers constantly off balance. He had a dark, brooding silence about him that called for others to be silent, too. Unsurprisingly, most didn't engage in frivolous conversation with Parker, for fear of being regarded as either a flake, a brown-nose, or simply ignorant about rowing.

If Parker didn't volunteer much information about the hows and whys of rowing, he was quick to correct inaccurate knowledge. And when faced with insubordination or foolish behavior, Parker's expression would become instantly grim—the long face would seem to grow longer—the eyebrows lifting in mock disbelief, the chin jutting out like a challenge, the lips pursing and often uttering a warning sound similar to the "Ho . . . " made by a Hollywood cowboy getting a horse to stop.

Parker had an unspoken protocol in the boathouse, some of which he had inherited from his own coach, Joe Burk, and one that he in turn passed on to others. It was an attitude that put stock in the theory that you should say less and do more. It frowned on ostentatious behavior, or anything that would embarrass the crew program or the college. Engaging an opponent in pre-race banter was largely taboo; talking on the water was a worse sin.

Harry Parker was a leader who obviously had a plan and a set of expectations, but he was not always going to share these with his athletes. Even on race day, when most coaches got up in front of their team and gave them an inspirational speech, or at least a few words of encouragement, Parker said virtually nothing—just a quick, pragmatic assessment of the race and how it should be rowed. Most athletes were mystified by his lack of words. Clint Allen, his varsity stroke in 1966, once approached his coach before a race and asked him if he wanted to tell him anything.

"No," was the reply. "You'll do fine."

And, left to his own devices, he did.

Some thought that part of this minimalist approach had to do with the singular population Parker had to deal with, the confident, often privileged pool of young Harvard oarsmen who crossed the river and dared to enter the huge, forbidding doors of Newell Boathouse. Although it was not always the case, many of the boys who entered Parker's world indeed came from affluent backgrounds and an exclusive gene pool. They were certainly bright young men who had been given the Harvard seal of approval, and provided they could make it through four years of study with respectable marks and no unseemly conduct, they had a promising future ahead of them. Few doors would ever be locked to them, least of all the doors of the boathouse.

Or so they thought until they met Parker.

Harry Parker wasn't there to coddle people, he was there to challenge them. Instead of having "feel good" team meetings, Parker would rather run sets of football stadiums with the team, encouraging them by direct example of his own physical prowess. And yet, he wasn't a drill sergeant either; he didn't force his Spartan philosophy on anyone. He expected his rowers to be able to think for themselves. More important than breeding or background was a necessary amount of self-confidence and discipline that no amount of coaching or training could instill. It was the same assuredness that Parker himself had, and you could see it readily in his crews.

But how would he act toward a group of strong-willed women?

WHILE PARKER WAS AWAY racing his varsity at Henley in early July, his former lightweight coach Steve Gladstone (now head coach at UCal Berkeley) was left in charge to look over the thirty-two recruits and recommend how to cut the number down to eighteen, or two eights worth. That way, when Parker returned, he would have a smaller, more qualified group from which to select the final nine.

Unlike Parker, who could be gruff and intimidating, Gladstone was a gregarious, handsome ex-rower who looked a little like Omar Sharif. When Carie Graves and Jackie Zoch had first seen him at Princeton, they had nudged each other, thinking he was cute. After two weeks of Gladstone, however, Carie realized that she actually preferred a coach who didn't talk so much and didn't try to tell her how to row. He also moved her back to the six seat, which she didn't particularly like because it meant having to follow other people.

There were a handful of other coaches helping out as well, and no one seemed to know exactly what was going on. They'd get the women out on the river and just have them row around for a while, sometimes racing them against each other in eights. The recruits were anxious to show what they could do, but no one had given them a definitive plan. After a while it became obvious that the assistant coaches were just biding their time until Parker returned, parading them up and down the Charles.

Gladstone himself had never seen such a group of strong women rowers, and was somewhat taken aback by their intensity. In terms of rowing experience, the group may have been young and unpolished, but they attacked the water without holding back. To Gladstone it was exciting and impressive to watch, a refreshing change from his normal dealings with oarsmen. One day he had the women do a series of grueling 1000-meter pieces, back-to-back. After they got off the water, Gladstone told them that he would never have been able to get a varsity men's crew to do that amount of work—the team would have told him to go to hell.

Then Parker returned, and everyone knew things would change. There would be no more messing around in boats.

BEYOND HARRY PARKER'S PERSONAL DOUBTS about coaching women lay the question of the ultimate potential of such an experimental group. On paper, at least, the odds did not look good. Parker would have less than two months to train a group of virtual rookies to go up against seasoned teams from countries like East Germany, Russia, and Romania, countries that took their women's rowing so seriously that individuals were selected for the sport at an early age, based on their genetic history and muscle type. The East Germans, especially, treated sports as a science and saw the benefit of herding the right type of bodies into the appropriate sport. For rowers, they looked for athletes who were tall, lean, and strong, with a great capacity for cardiovascular endurance.

Parker realized that he would inherit not only a hodgepodge of different body types, but also a group that had entirely different notions of how to row. And how did you train women anyway? What could they take in terms of hard work? Would they break down and cry, crack under pressure? Could he treat them the same dispassionate way he treated his Harvard team?

Gladstone's report had been favorable. And Parker had answered some of these questions himself when he'd worked with the recruits from the Eastern Development Camp that spring— the same ones who had come in third at the Nationals. This group included Wiki Royden, Gail Pierson, Sheila Dugan, Nancy Storrs, and a big, tall rower named Maggie MacLean, whom Steve Gladstone considered a shoe-in for the five seat. The strong work ethic of these women had impressed him, but he hadn't had the time or the energy to give them his full attention while Harvard was still in session.

The majority of the recruits were composed of various college stars like Carie Graves and her two teammates, Jackie Zoch and Sue Ela; two women from Yale named Anne Warner and Chris Ernst; the Princeton captain, Carol Brown, who stroked the U.S. National Team pair in 1974; Sharon Vassiere, a recent graduate of Boston University. The West Coast contingent was made up of two women from Cal State Long Beach, Claudia Schneider and Marty Ramos, and a sixteen-year-old coxswain from the ZLAC rowing club, an all-girls program named after its four founders: Zulette, Lena, Agnes, and Carolina. Baby-faced, blonde, and often barefoot, Lynn Silliman had come to the initial tryouts on a lark, and had cried openly when she'd made the first round of cuts—she hadn't planned on being away from home that long. Another coxswain from Radcliffe had arrived late, along with Wiki Royden,

Lynn Silliman, the sixteen-year-old coxswain.

ABOVE: Carie Graves, looking impatient *BELOW:* Claudia Schneider, the quiet rower from Long Beach, California.

ABOVE: Parker instructs from his launch. *BELOW: Seat Racing:* Anne Warner, Nancy Storrs, Jackie Zoch, Gail Ricketson, and Wiki Royden (far boat, right to left) go head-to-head with a crew led by Graves and Pierson, coxed by Lynn Silliman.

ABOVE: Parker beckons before the first shove for the finals at Nottingham.
BELOW: *"The Extra Balls Rowing Club":* Chris Ernst, Carol Brown, and
Nancy Storrs at bow, two, and three (left to right).

ABOVE: Moving away from the field in the repechages (U.S.A., top crew).
BELOW: Waiting for the clock's decision after the final of the World Championships (U.S.A., second from bottom).

Receiving silver medals at the awards dock.

A jubilant crew comes off the water.

After the Races: (Clockwise from upper left) Parker gives a rare smile; the two Yalies (Warner, Ernst) share a warm embrace; the unlikely crew poses modestly for a team photo (left to right: Warner, Silliman, Storrs, Graves, Schneider, Brown, Royden, Ernst and Pierson).

A Wanderer No Longer: Carie Graves walks alone at Land's End, England, after all the racing is over.

the Radcliffe stroke and sculler who had beaten Gail Pierson in her single.

They were, indeed, a motley bunch, but most of them shared one thing: a fresh perspective on a sport permeated by male tradition. Unlike most of the Harvard undergraduates who came through the doors at Newell, waiting for Coach Parker to make them into men, most of these women had already paid their dues. Most had not only experienced the normal rigors of rowing, but had also borne the additional hardships of being denied the basic privileges that came with it.

They hadn't just needed to walk into boathouses and prove themselves. They'd had to bang on the doors just to be let in.

Eight

ANNE WARNER, one of the two women from Yale, had knocked on Harry's door before. After her freshman year of crew, she had been so enthusiastic about the sport that she decided to continue rowing through the summer in a single scull. Because her family lived in the Boston area, she found her way to Weld Boathouse, where her Radcliffe rivals did their rowing. The Weld summer sculling program wasn't as strict about admitting only those affiliated with the college, but they did have some rules about boat usage.

Since she'd been a sweep rower, not a sculler, Anne had to begin by taking out wherries, wide lapstrake tubs that were slow and clunky but difficult to flip. After that, like other novice scullers, she moved through the categories of wide comps and narrow comps, before being allowed to row a club single. Once in the club boat, rowers had to race over a set four-mile course in less than thirty minutes to progress to the best racing singles—beautiful mahogany boats made by local builder Joseph Shea.

Anne quickly progressed through the various levels of boats at a speed that left the sculling attendant, Pete Galvin, baffled. Most novices took a few months, or even a few seasons, to move into a club single, and then twice as long to make it go fast enough to break the four-mile test. It took Anne Warner a couple of weeks.

Her sweep rowing at Yale had obviously helped, but there was more to it than that. It took a lot of skill to handle a narrow racing scull, and superb fitness to make it go under thirty minutes for four miles. Not many Harvard undergraduate men could even do it; it was a true test of strength, endurance, and sculling proficiency. Those who succeeded had their names entered into a special logbook and received a small commemorative medal. Anne didn't care about signing the book or getting the medal; she simply wanted to row in the best boat her ability would allow. But when she broke the thirty-minute test, Pete Galvin was at a loss about what to do—he hadn't planned on her being able to pass.

And so, in the end, he told her she would have to go across the river and get approval from Harry Parker.

PASSING THE SCULLING TEST hadn't been a big surprise to Anne Warner herself. Very early in her life, she'd discovered that she was both fast and powerful. After school, she hung out with some of the boys on her block, running and arm-wrestling with them for fun. Those who lost retaliated by calling her "muscles." Years later, sport physiologists would determine that her impressive muscles were almost exclusively made up of "fast-twitch" fiber, ideal for short, explosive power. But she wasn't really trying to impress anyone. All she knew was that she liked to *move*, and move vigorously. But there always seemed to be someone trying to prevent her from doing just that.

Her father was one of the only people aware of her physical needs, and he advised her to do some form of exercise for at least an hour every day when she went off to New Haven. Anne saw Yale as an opportunity to finally excel at some physical activity, and when they sent her an extracurricular interest survey the summer before her enrollment, she was so excited about all the choices that she checked off nearly every box. Finally, she'd be able to see what she could truly do.

The sports offerings in high school had been less than satisfactory, most of them too delicate, like dance, or watered-down versions of boys' sports. On the basketball team, for example, girls were required to play six, instead of five, to a team, with two players always remaining on defense in the inactive court. (This precluded the use of fast breaks, where a quick runner like Anne could excel.) Another silly rule stated that girl basketball players couldn't run more than three steps with the ball. Clearly, whoever had come up with these restrictions was afraid that rapid activity wasn't healthy for women.

When Anne complained about the rules and got into a fight with the girls' gym teacher, she was nearly kicked out of school. She'd yelled at the teacher and made some untoward remarks, but fortunately, the principal had intervened on Anne's behalf. He thought that despite her volatile delivery, Anne's comments were right on the mark.

Rowing, which demanded an enormous amount of energy, was a godsend for someone like Anne Warner. It let her use her body in a precise, yet powerful way. But even in rowing she found restrictions, an established hierarchy that needed to be challenged.

AT WELD that summer, Pete Galvin had not wanted her to row the good boats, and mumbled something about her not being a Harvard, or even a Radcliffe, student. When Anne kept pressing him, pointing out that she'd passed the required test, he finally told her that she'd have to get special permission from Coach Parker.

She'd heard about Harry Parker, as almost every rower had, but had never met him face-to-face. And when she walked over the Charles River and into the men's boathouse that first time, she was as intimidated as anyone would have been. She listened to each of her footfalls on the two flights of wide stairs leading up to Parker's office, noticed the framed posters from the '68 Mexico Olympics—where Parker had led his Harvard crew to their first appearance at the Olympics—and knocked on the door that was nearly always closed. Inside was a small room that resembled a sea captain's quarters, burdened by an oversized mahogany desk and lined with books.

Anne quickly explained her plight to Parker, talking in a rapid-fire manner that she often adopted when she got excited or nervous. Physical speed and power weren't her only natural gifts—she certainly hadn't gotten into Yale on an athletic scholarship. She was a Russian studies major and a musical composer, and her mind could operate at breakneck speed. Between high school and college, she'd composed and performed a dulcimer duet while working at WGBH in Boston (coincidentally, the piece was later used for a rowing recruiting video called *Symphony in Motion*, which she saw at a crew meeting her first day at Yale). Yet her goal was to achieve something extraordinary with her physical being, and she found herself always needing to justify this goal. When she explained her National Team and Olympic rowing plans to her Yale advisor, he simply shook his head and said:

"Go ahead, ruin your figure!"

Parker listened with his judge-like silence as she explained *everything*—not only that she had passed the sculling test, but that she felt it was important for her to train as hard and as well as she could, for there was talk of a U.S. women's camp in the offing. When she finished, he paused momentarily, mulling it over, and then said:

"Yes—I think you're absolutely right, I think you *should* row the senior singles!"

And that was it.

Anne almost couldn't believe her ears. It would have been so easy for him to shut her down, to tune her out, to simply shake his head and say no. What did he care about some young woman who didn't even go to Harvard? Instead, she sensed that this man had truly listened, had followed her own thought process, ambitions, and ability, and had come to the same logical conclusion.

"Do you need to call anyone?" Anne asked, tentatively.

"No," Parker said. "You just tell Pete that I said it was okay." He looked back down at whatever he was working on.

And from that moment on, she knew that she could trust Harry Parker, that he possessed the impartiality of a good judge.

THINGS AT YALE HAD certainly not gone this easily. The Ivy League schools, with their huge endowments, were actually some of the worst in terms of providing women access to proper facilities. Some had only recently allowed women to enroll as students and hadn't foreseen that they would also want to participate in sports. At Princeton, until her junior year, Carol Brown and her teammates had been largely forbidden from using the men's boathouse, only allowed access in the early morning hours to row, but forbidden from using the weight room or the bathrooms and showers. Anne Warner and Chris Ernst had been treated even worse at Yale.

Despite the new Title IX law passed in 1972, which required that universities dispense funds equally, most schools were slow to provide such equity. And crew was one of the more traditional sports. Aside from the issue of physical resources lay the attitude that women could never be serious competitive athletes in something that required such strength and sweat. Acceptable women's sports at the time included swimming, track and field, figure skating, and gymnastics.

The upshot was that a majority of the women entering Newell that summer, whatever their skill with an oar might be, were battle-hardened survivors. Many of them had been the first to bang on the door of men's boathouses until, begrudgingly or not, they'd finally been let in. Indeed, if a large part of rowing success came from perseverance, almost everyone who came to the Boston camp that summer had already pre-qualified as an able candidate for the eight.

And that was something Parker could use.

He'd studied the East German training methods and had developed his own theories about muscular strength and endurance, as well as efficient rowing technique. But in his mind these physiological factors were completely dependent on psychological ones, namely, that an oarsman had to really *want* to row, and be willing to train hard in order to succeed. This, in the end, was the bottom line. It went deeper than genetics, and was harder to gauge.

NOW THAT HARRY PARKER was standing in front of her again, welcoming the team, Anne felt reassured. Gladstone was a great coach, but he might not be able to make the leap of faith that was required here. To be successful, their leader had to look beyond the fact that they were women and treat them with equal deference and indifference. Things had been unclear the first few weeks of camp, as unpredictable as the odd, rainy weather. Usually Boston was hot and sunny in July, and the skies had been partly overcast for several days. Now that Parker had returned, everything quickly changed. He had already consulted with Gladstone and cut the number of candidates down from thirty-two to eighteen. There was no discussion about it, just a sheet of paper on the front door of the boathouse that morning.

The sun was shining again, turning the waters of the Charles from a gunmetal gray to a friendly shade of blue. It shone brightly on the faces of the remaining recruits, who sat in a rough semicircle on the gray dock outside the boathouse. Parker stood with his back to the river, holding a notebook in his left hand. He spoke to them in a deep voice, outlining his plan for the next several weeks. Ten rowers would be chosen and one coxswain; that ten would include two spares. Everyone, he said, would get a chance to earn a seat. He spoke slowly, clearly, and with an air of quiet confidence that comes with having done something many times before. Many of the rowers, who had been feeling skittish and stressed out, were suddenly put at ease, even when Parker freely admitted that he had never coached a group of women before and there would be some things he would have to figure out.

He was dressed casually in old running shoes and khaki shorts, but there was a sense of order and propriety about Parker, and an underlying intensity that shone clearly in his eyes. It was difficult to meet this gaze directly, and as if he knew this, he avoided sustained eye contact with them—preferring to stare down at the dock or at his notebook. At age forty, his hairline had already begun to recede, making his forehead and brow appear even more prominent. This, coupled with the slow, careful way he spoke, gave him the look of someone whose mind was in a state of constant calculation.

He was still in superb physical condition. The muscles in his forearms were heavily veined, jutting out past the rolled-up sleeves of his white shirt. His oversized quadriceps made his pants look too small. He was always fit, mentally and physically, like a drill sergeant who needed to hold himself up to his recruits as the example of what they could and should become. But it was the odd combination of mental edginess and silence that made him most distinct, made his Harvard guys give him nicknames like "Weird Harold," and "The Sphinx."

Despite his obvious doubts about coaching the group of women, Carie Graves liked him too. He exuded the same quiet confidence of her own coach, Jay Mimier. Looking at the other women, she could see that everyone had the same trust in Parker. He might be a little strange, but he would be honest and fair about the selection of the boat and not play personal favorites. A handsome, personable coach like Steve Gladstone might actually be a big problem among a group of women. Parker wasn't *unattractive*, he was just a little odd and aloof. And he wasn't going to let the fact that they were women get in the way of trying to win. In part of his speech, full of long, thoughtful pauses, he even ventured to suggest that the women recruits go on the pill to avoid what he incorrectly believed were the detrimental effects of the menstrual cycle—if it would help them at the Worlds.

As one of the rowers who had seen him in action, Gail Pierson had a similar trust, but a slightly different perspective. She knew that although Parker would talk very little to anyone personally, he would scrutinize each one of them with the careful eye of a jeweler—watch them from all angles, in different seats, and see who made a boat go fast. Beyond that, nothing really mattered to him, and when the time came to make a cut, he would do it in a cold, dispassionate way. He might cut her, despite their history together, despite everything she had done for women's rowing. In the end, Gail Pierson thought, Harry Parker would cut his own mother from a boat if he thought it would make it go faster.

Earlier that day, in fact, her friend Bernie Horton had bumped into one of the first casualties of the camp, a rower who certainly looked fit enough. Apparently, when she didn't see her name on the selection list that morning, she had gone in to question Parker about it. Now, the young woman was leaving the boathouse in tears, and when Bernie asked her what had happened, she explained that Parker had said that her rowing was simply too rough for him to correct in such short order. She should keep training and try again next year.

THE OTHER YALIE, Chris Ernst, lived in constant fear of being cut. At 5 feet 4 inches and 130 pounds, she was by far the smallest one to set foot in Newell and looked nothing like a rower should. Rowers were tall and lean, like Carie Graves, who had a body well designed to lever an oar through the water. Ernst was nearly a foot shorter than Carie; her head barely reached the Wisconsin stroke's shoulder. If not for the plucky swagger to her step and her well-defined muscles, Chris might indeed have been mistaken for a coxswain. And from the very start of the camp selection process, she knew that because of her size, other rowers and coaches would disregard her on sight, until she proved them wrong.

Outwardly, she gave no visible sign of worry. She was, instead, the one recruit who always seemed to be ready and willing for anything, a bundle of energy always chattering away, joking to herself and others. On one of the first days of camp, while everyone else wore their national team training shirts, Chris wore one that said, "Slippery when wet." She had a quick wit that often made light of what others considered tragic, and a big, broad smile that often spread over her round face, displaying most of her perfect teeth. It was a smile of almost childlike innocence, and it squeezed her eyes into twinkling half-moons.

It was the smile that stayed with you, that reminded you of the Cheshire cat. To look at Chris Ernst, you might easily get the impression that nothing bothered the diminutive rower, that life's problems were not only predictable, but altogether necessary. Only those who knew her a little better, like her teammate Anne Warner, might reveal that she was trying to make up for her size with an ebullient, big-hearted personality.

Anne Warner was not without her own sense of humor. On the first day of practice at the camp, Steve Gladstone had sent all the candidates on a two-mile, timed run around the Charles. It was a well-traversed loop, which began at Newell Boathouse and went quickly over the Anderson Bridge. Once on the Cambridge side of the river, the runners would head upstream for a mile, along the row of giant sycamores on Memorial Drive and past the Cambridge Boat Club, before they crossed back again at the Eliot Bridge. From there, it was less than a mile back to Newell.

Gladstone had sent hundreds of rowers on this two-mile loop when he had been the lightweight coach at Harvard. Running was a standard, basic test of fitness that almost every crew coach used from time to time, especially when the water was unrowable. That day, the morning after the fourth of July, the river was so overrun with powerboats that he'd decided to keep them on dry land. Running was not, of course, an accurate measure of one's rowing prowess, and some oarsmen thought it was just a waste of time.

Whatever she did, Anne Warner liked to win. In this respect, she wasn't different from anyone else on the run; they were all highly competitive individuals. But Anne also had a sense of playfulness that sometimes expressed itself in prankish behavior. And if she found a contest inherently unfair, the odds stacked against her, she would often find a way to simply change the rules.

Recently, the team had gone out to dinner together at a Greek restaurant, and she had challenged Wiki Royden to a baklava-eating contest. Royden was the Radcliffe stroke, her arch Ivy League rival, but at the camp the two had quickly become friends. Still, when it became apparent that Wiki was going to win, Anne secretly scooped the baklava into her lap. She didn't tell Wiki about it until a few days later.

Not far into the team run, Anne decided it might be more fun to simply cut the course by swimming across the Charles at the halfway mark. She persuaded Wiki and Carol Brown, both excellent swimmers, to join her, and the three of them swam the width of the river. They emerged on the Cambridge side, not far from the boathouse, and ran in well ahead of the others. Steve Gladstone hadn't been fooled for too long. It was hot out, but not enough to drench the three rowers in sweat. He immediately made them rerun the course, this time accompanying them to make sure they would finish. Even so, he thought their prank was pretty funny.

Some of the other rowers weren't so easily amused.

Anne Warner was the stroke of the Yale crew, and had the independent, high-spirited nature of a good leader. Chris Ernst admired how she could be openly combative about things that bothered her, but also noticed how she was deeply affected by those things she could not change. Once, while they were both sitting in a Yale boat during practice, Anne had gotten into such a heated argument with their coxswain that the entire crew had needed to stop rowing. No one really knew what the argument was about, but when Anne removed her oar from the oarlock, they figured it was pretty serious. For a moment, in fact, it looked like Anne might actually try to hit the coxswain over the head with it. Whether this was actually the case, or whether the twelve-and-a-half-foot-long oar simply proved too long for her to wield as a club, no one really knew. In the end, she simply pitched it out of the boat, refusing to row another stroke. The Yale coach, Nat Case, finally retrieved the oar and threw it back into Anne's lap. The crew then resumed its practice.

Yes, Anne Warner could be as intense as any stroke, but most of the stories about her were amusing in retrospect, tales of a passionate young woman with a strong will and a highly developed intellect.

But there was one story that wasn't funny and that would never seem so, even years after her rowing days had ended. Neither Chris nor Anne would ever forget the feeling of humiliation that overcame them as young rowers at Yale, when they had gone to the campus weight room to train. The Yale men hadn't ever seen women lift weights before and had lined up along the upper balcony of the gymnasium and leered at them, calling them names to make them leave.

Collectively, Chris Ernst and Anne Warner had experienced some of the worst treatment of the entire group in Boston, although it wasn't altogether atypical. As part of the first flight of women admitted to Yale, they had become guinea pigs for the college's experiment in coeducation. On paper, perhaps, the Ivies were ready to admit women. In practice, however, they were somewhat unprepared. They had not foreseen all the liberties and privileges the women would expect to have.

The oversights ranged from not equipping certain buildings like the chemistry department with women's bathrooms, to not having enough living space on campus. Dorm life had always been an important part of the Yale experience, a way of welcoming its new students and encouraging camaraderie among the members of each incoming class. However, because of the housing shortage, Chris had spent her first fall semester living off campus in the city of New Haven. But the worst treatment came when the women expressed a desire to participate in crew and other athletic programs that had formerly been the sole province of Yale men.

As the oldest and most distinguished of the intercollegiate sports, crew was one of the cornerstones of athletics at Yale, rivaling Harvard in the number of victories and distinguished oarsmen it had produced. Benjamin Spock, the famed child psychologist, had pulled an oar for Yale and won an Olympic gold medal in Paris in 1924. Cole Porter, another Yale graduate, had even written a song about Yale Crew.

Porter's song appeared in a 1914 campus show called *Paranoia*, and its lyrics lightly mocked the self-inflated status of the Yale oarsman. Yet the Yale varsity rowers were indeed seen as icons of American sport. Their wholesome image appeared everywhere, from kids' comic books to playing cards, so who could blame them?

By the time Chris Ernst and Anne Warner set foot on the New Haven campus, rowing at Yale was well over 100 years old, having begun in New Haven harbor as early as the 1850s. With the inception of the Harvard–Yale race in 1857, both colleges had pushed each other and refined the art of competitive rowing until they both came to represent symbols of the finest amateur rowing in America. Their annual duel, held in New London, Connecticut, perpetuated the grandness of their image, both in the rowing community and around the world.

In the heyday of Yale rowing, when Cole Porter penned his song, thousands turned out on the Thames River in early June each year, just to see Harvard and Yale do battle over the four-mile course. The competition was patterned after the famous Oxford–Cambridge boat race in England, and if nothing else it was an exclusive event, both for the participants and for those who watched them. By 1914, there were two trains and two steam launches for spectators, with tickets often running above the five-dollar asking price. Those with private yachts got the best view, either by following the race or mooring near the finish line. A well-heeled crowd was often in attendance. J. P. Morgan sometimes watched the festivities from his steam launch, the *Corsair*, taking in the race before attending his annual Harvard reunion.

Although it was touted as a strictly amateur affair, betting often took place among the spectators. The odds changed from year to year, based on the coaching staff, the size of the athletes, and the rowing style adopted by each crew. For over 100 years, the Harvard–Yale race had been a fairly even contest, with neither crew winning more than ten times in succession. On five occasions, in fact, the tally of victories had stood dead even, and in 1962, when Harry Parker took the helm for Harvard, the tally stood nearly even again.

Then Yale began to lose. And lose again. By the time Chris Ernst and Anne Warner began rowing in 1973, the men in blue had lost eleven straight, and were due to keep losing for another five years.

Some thought the losses were due to Parker's wizardry; others thought it was a reflection of the times. After two world wars and the Vietnam conflict, college rowing was no longer as popular as it had once been, the Yale oarsman no longer the shining symbol of success. The '60s were a time for students to break from traditional pursuits, and it was more stylish for men to have long hair and hold a folk guitar than it was to have a crew cut and hold an oar. For many women, however, it was the other way around.

In any case, Yale rowing had fallen on hard times. Varsity rowers who put in an enormous amount of time training were lucky to win a handful of races by the time they graduated. Beating Harvard in New London was a pipe dream. It was a depressing time to be a varsity oarsman at Yale. And it was in this climate that the first women rowers set out to make a name for themselves.

THE YALE BOATHOUSE was located in Derby on the Housatonic River, a thirty-minute drive from the New Haven campus. Built in the 1920s out of cinder blocks and stucco, it was a more modest structure than either of the two Harvard boathouses, about half the size and without the elaborate ornamentation. The Housatonic River, too, in addition to being far away from campus, was much narrower than the Charles and had fewer stretches of straight open water on which to conduct training and racing. When Yale lost to Harvard, some pointed to the lesser facility as part of the reason why the Elis were at a deficit.

The original Yale boathouse was much nearer to campus, situated at the mouth of the Quinnipiac River, where it emptied into Long Island Sound. Soon after the boathouse was built, however, the waterway became a crowded and polluted industrial thoroughfare and had to be abandoned for higher ground. The old boathouse was turned into an office building, and all that remained to store boats nearby was a small Quonset hut standing in a swampy inlet. And this is where, for their very first efforts, the Yale women were brought to row. For equipment, they were issued the huge, oversized eights originally built for Yale's intramural rowing program, known affectionately as battalion or "bat" boats. At least ten rowers were required to carry the heavy shells on and off the water.

The women's coach, Nat Case, had been a Yale oarsman, and so had his father and brother before him. Like Carie Graves' coach, Jay Mimier, he basically worked on a volunteer basis, with very little pay from the college. Like Mimier, he trained the women's squad hard, as he had been trained, and when they began to look like a real crew and win races, he decided to bring them out to Derby. There, they borrowed an old, discarded men's boat, and attached blocks of wood to the feet in order to take full strokes. The boat was still too big for the women.

The move to Derby was not welcomed by the Yale men, who saw the women as an intrusion to a place and a program that had been exclusively theirs for generations. Case himself had mixed emotions about his role in this. On the one hand, he wanted his women's team to do well; on the other, he didn't want to be ostracized by his fellow Yalies as the infidel who disturbed the sanctity of Yale Crew. He did his best not to interfere with the men. And when it was announced that his paltry salary would not be increased one spring, he wasn't going to fight about it. He told the women that he'd probably have to take a better paying job at the University of Washington.

Chris Ernst and Anne Warner couldn't believe he'd go without a fight. Teary-eyed, they decided that an unscheduled visit to the Yale president's house was needed. Unfortunately, Kingman Brewster wasn't there, but his wife listened carefully to all they had to say and promised to relay their concerns to her husband. When Nat Case found out about the visit, he was not pleased. He didn't like to do things so aggressively. The result, however, was that he not only got a decent salary that spring, but a brand new women's eight as well.

Getting things done at Derby was a different matter. Case had to shuttle the new boat back and forth on his Volkswagen bus, because he was not allowed to store it inside the men's boathouse. The women were allowed to ride the campus shuttles with the men's team, but this was actually a negative experience.

After practice, when the women came off the river, they had to pile straight onto the shuttle bus. They were not allowed to use the boathouse showers or the bathrooms. Cold and sweaty in the chilly months of fall and spring, the women waited until the men had taken their hot showers and joined them for the long ride back to school. Most of the Yale men seemed unconcerned about the women's plight, and some barely even acknowledged their female counterparts. They did, however, take note of their comings and goings off the bus; the places where women were let off were known as "crack stops."

WHEN CHRIS ERNST FIRST WENT OUT for crew as a sophomore, Nat Case had not been very impressed. In addition to being exceptionally small, Ernst had shown up with a bandaged knee, the result of a nagging gymnastics injury. Although she'd yearned to play various other sports her entire life, gymnastics had been one of the few athletic opportunities open to her. Now, with the knee problem, she needed to find something new.

Case immediately placed her in the second boat, assuming that she was too small to contribute much power. Then one day, he decided to do some erg testing in order to better measure the strength of the squad. Each rower would do three, two-minute-long pieces. When Ernst posted one of the top scores on the first piece, Case added more weight to the basket that controlled how much load went on the oar handle. The greater the amount of weight in the basket, the more the erg favored someone who themselves weighed more. A bigger person could simply hang their greater mass on the oar handle and generally get a better score. But even with the added weight, Ernst again scored well. How was it possible, Case wondered, that such a tiny person could pull that much harder than the others?

Much of Ernst's strength came from her upper body, which she had developed over several years of gymnastics. She had also developed a sense of what it meant to fight for recognition. In high school, the boys' and girls' gymnastics teams had sometimes needed to share the same space and equipment. Often they clashed over the use of the gym. There, as at Yale, the boys didn't want to share. When this happened, however, instead of just complaining about it, Chris came up with a sporting way to settle the issue: she suggested that she arm-wrestle the boys for use of the gym.

Those who accepted her challenge were as surprised as Nat Case had been, when Ernst beat them almost every time. Defeat, not decorum, finally forced them to yield the floor.

WHEN THE YALE WOMEN'S CREW BEGAN winning most of their races, however, their lot still didn't improve. They'd still been forbidden to use the men's boathouse. In the fall, they'd gotten a temporary trailer to change in, but then in the spring, the college had forgotten to secure the permit for it. Now, as Chris Ernst was oft to say to her teammates, they didn't even have a pot to piss in.

Chris and Anne complained to the women's athletic director, who said she'd look into it, but right now there just wasn't enough money to build a women's facility. The truth of it was, women's issues aside, crew had always been a thorn in the side of college athletic departments, and this sentiment had only gotten worse. Boats and boathouses cost a lot of money and, compared to other sports, crew brought in very little revenue. Money, however, wasn't really the issue.

But some day soon, she promised them, changes would be made. Meanwhile, they waited on the shuttle bus every morning, feeling the icy sweat melt back into their skin.

N i n e

~~~~~~~

THE LIFE OF A CREW COACH wasn't an easy one, despite how it might look to someone glancing out of the car window in the morning, stuck in rush-hour traffic on the riverbanks. Many might look longingly at the pastoral scene they saw on the Charles River and envy what they envisioned as the life of a coach—a life spent out in the open air, motoring up and down the river trailing after their crews. Compared to the prospect of being cooped up in an office, piloting a launch and watching a group of people row might indeed seem like a pleasant enough way to spend one's days.

The reality, of course, was quite different. True, a crew coach like Harry Parker did get to work outside and drive around in a motor launch. But for Parker a launch was just a tool for his work and wasn't treated like a pleasure craft. The only real thought a coach ever gave to his launch was whether it was functioning properly, and whether it had enough gas to make it through practice. Likewise, the river was just a body of water on which his crews worked, not a scenic backdrop for the coach's or the rowers' pleasure. For some time now, in fact, the Charles had become much too polluted to swim in. If an oarsman happened to fall in the water, Harvard health services required confirmation of a recent tetanus shot. But even if the Charles *had* been a pristine environment, it wouldn't have changed much for a coach like Parker. He was too wrapped up in the details surrounding one objective: winning races.

What an outsider usually also failed to notice was that coaches and their crews were often on the river well before sunrise, rowing in weather that most people would find less than ideal. In late fall and early spring, the wind chill made veteran coaches like Parker dress up like longshoremen, in bulky jackets, insulated boots, and a wool watch cap. Even during the summer, on cloudy days, they kept a set of foul-weather gear handy in the event of sudden rain. Crews went out in everything but lightning or heavy winds.

Although a crew coach wasn't out on the water round the clock, like some fishermen were, Parker would often go out three or four times a day in the middle of peak racing season, for two to four hours a session. And most of that time would be spent concentrating very hard on what lay in front of him, not enjoying the unique combination of natural beauty and cityscape offered by the Charles.

Bill Miller, who was a launch driver at Harvard for a while (before he became a coach at Boston University), observed that the concentration of a good coach was quite intense. Crew coaching, he thought, required an effort equal to, if not greater than, any of the athletes in the boat. A two-hour session on the water could leave you drained of energy, even though you hadn't taken a single stroke yourself. And Parker, he noticed, was often out on the Charles for several hours a day coaching several crews, fall, spring, and summer. In addition to this, unlike most other coaches, Parker still found the time to work out himself, either to row his single or to run stadiums alongside his athletes. Miller could never fathom where he got his boundless energy, why he never seemed to burn out.

COACHING FROM A LAUNCH was a sometimes cumbersome but necessary way to groom a crew. Before gas-fired engines were available, some coaches used bicycles or even sculled alongside their crews. These forms of locomotion had their obvious deficiencies. The single scull might be handy to demonstrate technique to a novice crew, but an experienced boat could easily outrow a single. Coaching from a bicycle might be a little better, depending on the condition of the path along the river and its proximity to the water. On the Charles, however, the bike paths were shielded from the river by a thin wall of trees in many places, making this option impractical. A launch was the only way to do the job well.

A launch allowed a coach to view his crew from all angles, to examine it with a casual but careful eye. He could follow directly behind the crew, to check the timing of all the port, and then the starboard, oars. This was the coxswain's perspective, and from here it was easy to see if the blades were going in and out of the water together, or if one of them was slightly off at the catch. From here you could also study the boat's balance, whether it was "set up" solidly in between strokes, or whether it tended to dip down to one side.

A good coxswain could take care of these matters for you, the balance and the bladework, so that you could motor up alongside the crew to get a better look at the rowers themselves—not only how well they were swinging into the bow together and preparing their upper bodies for the next stroke, but more subtle, finer nuances such as how they were holding their arms and wrists. For this reason, it was very important for a coach to get someone good in the coxswain's seat very quickly, even before the rest of the crew was selected. A good coxswain allowed a coach to get about his other business without worrying whether the crew was going to hit a bridge. But first, of course, a coxswain had to know how to steer.

You couldn't really teach someone how to do this; it was something that came by feel, or it didn't. There were simply too many variables at work, all coming into play at the same time. Not only did a coxswain have to deal with the effects of wind and current on the boat, and discrepancies in the power of the rowers, but she also faced the more basic fact that there were no road maps or even buoys on most rivers. Constant dead reckoning was required.

For all of these reasons, coxing an eight was much harder than driving a car. It was much more like flying a small airplane. You had to gauge the weather around you and the speed of your craft to predict, ahead of time, how to adjust your course. You had to know that it was much easier to land the boat going into a head wind than a tail wind, that despite the added difficulty for the oarsmen, it helped set the boat up and keep its point and balance. If you botched a landing, it generally meant damaging the fragile bow of the shell, possibly ruining the boat for the next day's practice.

Parker himself knew the Charles River better than even a river boat pilot would have to know it, not only where the current ran the strongest and the various water depths, but also the shortest path along a certain stretch of river and how the wind would affect speed over that section. Even more precisely and to the amazement of a young coxswain, he could tell them exactly what "point" or mark they had to begin with to eventually end up on the right course.

These perceptions weren't obvious to every coach, they were proven by keen observation and keeping journals. It was his business to know the river and its daily ways, just as it was a stock broker's business to open up the paper every morning and have a sense of what was happening on Wall Street. He took his job very seriously. This familiarity with the river paid off during local races, when his intimate knowledge of the Charles gave his crew a major advantage.

LYNN SILLIMAN, the baby-faced sixteen-year-old from California, had taken to the coxswain's seat with the bearing of an old pro. First and foremost, she had the ability to steer the sixty-foot shell using a rudder not much larger than her outspread hand. On the Charles, which had once been named "winding path" by the local Abenaki Indians, a coxswain couldn't steer by the rudder alone. She had to know how and when to employ the rowers on port and starboard to help negotiate the bigger turns. But the women recruits had noticed much more than Lynn's ability to navigate.

Added to all this steering business was the task of handling the rowers, of telling them not only when to row but how, what pressure they should be pulling and what the stroke rating was, and whether or not they were rushing forward too quickly for the next stroke. The stern of the boat, where the coxswain sat, was like the back of an airplane in terms of its sensitivity. More so than any of the rowers, a coxswain felt the disruptions in the boat's balance and forward glide. A good coach could see a little of this from outside the boat, but his vision couldn't match the coxswain's sensitivity or what some of the rowers felt in the boat.

Lastly, beyond steering and commanding a crew, the coxswain had the responsibility of motivating the rowers to row hard and well. With a coach like Parker, who did so little talking, the coxswain had to be able to take up the slack. Could a sixteen-year-old, with only a semester of coxing behind her, really take control of this group of women, most of whom were ten years older and a foot taller than she was? Could she handle sitting face-to face with someone like Carie Graves or Anne Warner, who could reduce an incompetent cox to tears? Whoever sat in the seat had to be able to hold her own with anyone, and that wasn't done with the rudder but with the mouth.

A crew didn't like a total chatterbox in the stern, someone who upbraided them for every false move. Nor did they favor a cox who said absolutely nothing. A coxswain, after all, was their eyes in a race and had to tell them where they were and when to move through or hold back another crew. If the cox talked too much, the rowers would simply tune her out and stop listening. They'd do the same thing, or worse, if she made bad judgment calls or didn't steer the boat straight. With a bad coxswain, the rowers were always wondering whether the balance was off because of someone's poor technique or simply because of bad steering. And when they began to sense the latter, they would tense up every time they approached a bridge or another boat.

In the end, a coxswain was accepted by a crew based on doing all of these things well, so that the rowers could focus on their rowing and not have to think much at all. But a coxswain's role involved more than just becoming the brains of the boat. A good cox became its collective spirit, and could say and do things that were not only wise, but that addressed the emotional state of the crew. When rowers were tired or feeling down, the coxswain had to find a way to bring them up; when they were jittery or nervous, she had to settle them down. And in a race itself, she had to be aggressive, had to verbally diminish the stature of the other crew so that her boat had the confidence to mow them down.

Could a sixteen-year-old do this? Parker wondered. Two other coxswains had tried out for the eight, and both had more racing experience than Lynn. One, however, couldn't steer at all, and the other was having serious problems with her weight. Because a cox didn't physically contribute to the boat, it was better if they weighed as little as possible. With her elfin build, Lynn was a natural 98 pounds, a good deal under the allowable 120. But could she stare a German or a Russian opponent down at the starting line of the World Championships? He got his answer one day when he tried to question the exactness of her steering.

"Lynn, keep on course!" he called out, using his big, hand-held megaphone with the crimson "H" on it.

A lot of other coaches used electronic megaphones, to ensure that their crews heard everything they said. Parker's voice was so deep and strong that it didn't need amplification. With just a slight modulation of tone, he could instill either confidence or fear in a crew, or chastise a young coxswain and reduce her to a quiet, quivering mass in the stern. But this one wasn't so easily intimidated.

"I *am* on course!" Lynn shouted back.

"I'm sorry, Lynn, but you're not . . ."

"Yes, I *am!*"

Parker hesitated. Yes, this one would do.

The team certainly had confidence in her. When it came to selecting the coxswain, many coaches asked the rowers what they thought of the different candidates. "I think the choice is pretty obvious," Anne Warner told Harry. When he asked her why, she explained that Lynn was fresh, articulate, and feisty, attributes shared by the crew itself. Parker nodded, knowing exactly what she meant. Yes, most of the time the choice of coxswain was pretty obvious.

Choosing the right rowers was another matter.

THE CENTRAL AND MOST OBVIOUS task for a crew coach was to select and develop, to criticize and cajole, the eight rowers who powered the boat. This process was an art in itself, a skill akin to selecting an eight-piece orchestra and getting them to play together. There were certain general rules or guidelines that every coach followed, which had to do with first measuring the skill and power of the rowers and then judging where in the boat they should sit.

In a very general sense, crew was not unlike baseball, a sport that Parker also loved and that he had played in high school, before taking up rowing. Boston was in the middle of another season of baseball fever—its favorite summer sport. The Red Sox were doing well again; they'd just gotten the best of the Yankees in a four-game series, led by veteran Carl "Yaz" Yastrzemski and a group of rookies, including Carlton Fisk and Fred Lynn.

It took nine men to play baseball, and it took nine people to make up a crew—eight rowers and a coxswain. In baseball, each player had very specific skills. In rowing, while it looked like every-one in the boat was doing exactly the same motion, each seat in fact had its own unique character. To the outsider, these differ-ences were imperceptible, but to a coach, the seating of a boat was one of the keys to its success. In this sense a crew coach had the same challenge as any team sport coach—to select the right people and put them in the right positions.

In baseball, the coach already knew where to put the athletes. A shortstop was a shortstop, a first baseman was a first baseman. Players trained for specific positions and generally couldn't be switched around too much. Carlton Fisk was a catcher and would always be a catcher. Carl Yastrzemski could probably play any posi-tion in the outfield, but he sure couldn't pitch. In rowing the differ-ences were a lot more subtle and required a better eye to ascertain.

In sweep rowing, the only thing that was initially set in stone was what side a rower was on, port or starboard. It was as difficult for most oarsmen to row both sides as it was for a baseball player to be a switch hitter, to be able to swing from either side of the plate. The reason for this was basically the same in both sports. The left and right hands did slightly different things as they took a stroke, or a swing, and the body learned to be more coordinated on one side or the other.

In rowing, it was the "inboard hand"—the one nearest to the blade—that was responsible for feathering, or turning the blade between strokes. Feathering, of course, allowed the blade to travel backward toward the bow with less resistance from either wind or water. The "outboard hand" was the one positioned nearer the end of the oar handle. Being closer to the end of the giant-sized lever of the oar, it had more potential to help move the oar through the water. The outboard arm was the oarsman's power arm. As such, ports overdeveloped the left side of their backs, and starboards the right side; over time, the twisting unevenness of the sweep rowing motion could put an actual twist in an oarsman's spine.

Gail Pierson, the sculler and the oldest rower in the group, had chosen to be a starboard sweep rower. Her boyfriend, Sy Cromwell, had encouraged her to row starboard—told her she'd have a better shot at making the team there. Part of this, he explained, was because most people were right-handed and found it more difficult to learn to feather with their left hand. As a sculler, Gail had learned to feather equally well with both hands, so this would not be a problem.

The second reason to row starboard was that more people tended to row port simply because the lead rower normally sat on the port side. For some arbitrary reason, most sweep boats were rigged with a port stroke, and when new recruits found this out, they all wanted to row port and have a shot at the stroke seat. It was simply an ego thing.

Carie Graves was a port, so were Anne Warner and Wiki Royden, all strokes from their respective programs, and all extroverts with strong personalities. Carol Brown from Princeton wasn't a stroke, but she was the team captain. Jackie Zoch, Carie's teammate, was equally outspoken. (One time, back in Wisconsin, she had made the outrageous comment, loud enough for all to hear, "I think I'm actually stroking the boat from the four seat.")

Gauging the strength of each rower was much trickier than it looked. Many coaches got excited by an athlete's size and favored those who stood over six feet tall. But a big person could actually be weak, or ineffective at moving water. Their extra weight then became a detriment to a boat, and they were soon referred to by the other rowers as an "anchor." Conversely, a small person might really know how to use her body, to apply every ounce of her strength to the oar.

Some of these assessments could be done by eye. Parker and Steve Gladstone had done this initially, weeding out those who clearly weren't pulling that hard or were so hapless with an oar that they disrupted the boat. Both strength and style could be corrected over time, but Parker didn't have the spare time to do this.

Given the wide range of ability in the original thirty-two recruits, he and Gladstone had begun with this casual method of inspection. But some things were more difficult to see and had to be tested. Steve Gladstone, for example, had originally disregarded Chris Ernst on the basis of her size. Later, this quick judgment had proven incorrect.

A more "scientific" assessment of strength could be done by testing each rower on the ergometers. Nat Case, who also assisted Parker during the first week of camp, had used the erg at Yale to uncover the true value of Chris Ernst. But even the erg was, in fact, not entirely accurate. It was a pretty good gauge of an athlete's cardiovascular ability, but it showed nothing about either their skill with an oar or how well they could row in synchronicity with others. Oarsmen referred to these second two qualities as "smoothness." A smooth rower blended in so well with the rest of the crew that they were often overlooked, or at least undervalued.

Claudia Schneider was a classic example of a smooth rower. Tall and lean with more of a runner's build, she had never expected to be chosen for the camp. Her coach at Long Beach State was surprised when Parker had selected her at Princeton, along with two other rowers from her boat. The Long Beach Crew hadn't done all that well at the Nationals, hadn't even made the final. But clearly Parker had seen something that he liked.

Now three weeks of the camp had gone by, and Claudia was the only Californian to survive the next round of cuts—she and Lynn Silliman. As before, Parker had silently posted a single sheet of yellow lined paper on the front door of the boathouse, with the names of those selected scrawled in pen. He walked away and said nothing else. People gathered around, and either jumped for joy or quickly skulked away. Anne Warner was so pleased about Lynn Silliman that she grabbed the coxswain's lithe body and hoisted it over her shoulder. Then, after everyone had dispersed, Claudia took down the yellow sheet of paper and brought it back to her dorm room. There, she looked it over again and again. Why had she made it over the other Long Beach women, the ones her own coach had thought were better? Or why, for that matter, had she moved past so many of the other East Coast rowers who came from superior rowing programs?

Like Carie Graves, Claudia came from a program that rowed in virtual isolation. The Long Beach boathouse was shaped like a shoe box, and the team rowed around on the ocean in a bay near Naples Island. Claudia was in awe of the East Coast rowing establishment, which had such a strong sense of history and tradition. Back at Long Beach, crew had been a lot more casual. They worked just as hard, but the attitude was different. Winning was not such a big deal.

Claudia was used to being thrown into a boat and left to figure things out for herself. During her very first day of crew practice, the coach had been short one athlete and had put her in a boat with no instruction whatsoever. After a long, frustrating row where she committed every faux pas in the book—crabbing, hitting other women in the back with her oar—she was at her wit's end. She was also exhausted, and it looked like they were rowing further and further away from the dock. Just as she was about to collapse, they arrived back home.

It turned out that they had actually rowed around in a big circle.

After two days in bed and a vow never to return, she found herself back at the Long Beach boathouse. She was smitten with crew, despite the travesty of her first outing. Like Carie, she had found a sport that challenged her down to the core. Unlike Carie, however, Claudia was a listener and a follower. Anytime a coach said *anything* to *anyone* she would listen and try to apply the comments to her own rowing. Back in Princeton, when Parker had briefly coached her Cal boat during the selection process, she had immediately tried to grasp the different style that he was preaching and modify her own stroke to match it.

She had smooth, long strokes to match her easygoing personality. But the remaining eighteen recruits were starting to get really competitive. How could she prove herself among such a group? When Parker put her on the ergometers and she scored rather poorly, she suspected that she might not make the final cut. She hated the ergs and didn't fare well on them. No, there had to be another way to prove herself, and she approached Parker to find out what that was.

IN THE END there was only one way to really test oarsmen, and it wasn't on the rowing machines.

Parker had discovered the only proper way, a few summers earlier, while he and Steve Gladstone were coaching a men's national team eight out of Union Boat Club. It was called seat racing, and it involved breaking up an eight into two separate fours, then racing different groupings of oarsmen against one another. Some people thought this was a sadistic version of musical chairs, an all-out war among the people in the boat, but in the end the top eight people would generally self-select.

Making these decisions was the real chore of the crew coach, to look deeply into the souls of the athletes and identify those who had not only the right build or the right cardiovascular system, but also the killer instinct. A coach couldn't give this sort of thing to an athlete, but he could certainly draw it out where it might be lying dormant. Sometimes it was easy to detect, sometimes it was hiding behind a polished, smiling exterior.

Women, Parker decided, shouldn't be treated any differently. Male or female, once rowers were pitted against each other, against pain, it was pretty easy to read their faces and see who was digging in and who was checking out.

And that's where seat racing came in handy.

T e n

~~~

MAGGIE MACLEAN was just the sort of rower that Carie Graves couldn't tolerate, one who didn't seem to handle the hardships of rowing well. First she had complained to Harry about having her period, and he had given her a day off. Then she got tendonitis, a result of rowing incorrectly, and he had given her a week-long reprieve. Finally, when she returned, her hands had grown so soft that they immediately became blistered and chewed up on the coarse wooden oar handles. Every stroke she took, her hands were in pain, despite the bandages and the gloves that she now wore.

Real rowers didn't wear gloves; they also didn't take time off. Maggie could feel the resentment building up against her from some of the other rowers who felt she wasn't tough enough, despite being one of the bigger rowers at the camp. The health services at Harvard were little help; they simply told her not to row at all. When they first treated her for tendonitis, they had been sympathetic, but when she returned with her hands looking like ground beef, they shook their heads and said, "You don't belong here, you should be up on the fourth floor—Psychiatric!"

What they didn't understand was that the standards of conduct for oarsmen were different from those of the average person. Unless a rower was nearly on death's doorstep, she was expected to show up for practice every day. If this seemed like an overly macho attitude, it had a very practical basis too. Unlike most other team sports, where a missing player could generally be replaced without great loss, an absent rower might mean the boat could not function properly. It was like a bird with a broken wing.

And Maggie's arm was definitely in bad shape now. They shot it full of cortisone and put it in a temporary cast.

The injury or absence of a star football, baseball, or basketball player could greatly impact the performance of those teams, too, but a missing rower from any seat in the boat sometimes meant the boat couldn't go on the water. For better or worse, most college rowing programs carried no "spares," no alternate rowers who waited around for a chance to substitute. When an injury or an illness did occur, a crew could try to borrow a member from another squad, like the freshman boat, but that provided only a temporary fix. Someone would then need to replace the missing freshman.

Beyond these logistics was the simple fact that when a crew had learned to row together, it was truly a single organism, with eight appendages and one brain—the coxswain. Given time, each member began to physically mesh with one another and achieve the balance, power, and rhythm of the whole boat. Replacing one of the crew members meant readjusting all of these subtle calibrations.

Mentally, too, knowing that a member of the crew would pull hard on race day, in spite of some unexpected illness or injury, was essential to developing the inner trust of a boat. When rowers talked about this trust they weren't talking about morals. Trust had nothing to do with personal integrity, religious beliefs, or political opinions outside the boat. Instead, it was a simple, shared expectation that when you sat down in your seat and tied into your shoes, you were committed, body and soul, to the boat. Like

Odysseus and his crew as they rowed past the sirens, you had to block out the alluring call of anything outside the boat, put wax in your ears and blinders on your eyes, and not let anything interfere with your forward progress. And no matter what happened, you never stopped rowing hard.

Every good crew had its stories of a rower who blacked out from the pain at the completion of a hard race, or rowed through a bad injury or a trick knee. In order to do this, you had to live by a code which suggested that your own personal senses and thoughts were less trustworthy or valid than those of the crew. Pain due to exhaustion was the most obvious deceiver, but there were plenty of other distractions and weaknesses—always an excuse if you wanted to find one.

Maggie's problems, although perfectly acceptable in the everyday world, could not be tolerated by such a highly competitive group. When a crew suspected weakness from a potential team member, it could turn on that person in an instant. The weak member of the crew would be ostracized unless the coach intervened and made the cut quickly himself.

But Parker seemed to be dragging out the decision, providing Maggie with every opportunity to redeem herself. Carie and Jackie couldn't figure it out. Last week he'd trimmed the team down to ten people and two "conditionals"—Maggie and Lauren Shealy. Shealy had injured her arm so badly that she'd recently decided to leave the camp. Maggie, however, was still hanging on. Wiki Royden had gotten tendonitis, too, and had taken the week off with Maggie, the two running stadiums together to keep in shape. Now, they were both going to be put back in the boat to see if they had healed up or not.

But something had happened during their week off. The team had already begun to bond as a result of the intense work, and close ranks against those who hadn't taken part. Maggie had always felt a little excluded from the circle of college rowers, many of whom had come to the camp with a teammate in tow and a host of good rowing memories. Jackie and Carie, Ann and Chris—they could support one another through difficult times.

Maggie and Wiki had rowed together in the EDC boat that came in second at the Nationals, and there were certainly some good memories between them. Maggie had rowed behind Wiki in the five seat, and she had made Wiki wash her lucky shorts before the final because they smelled so rank. Then, of course, they had come in third, losing to both Wisconsin and Vesper. She assumed Wiki had forgiven her for that, but now she too seemed withdrawn and distant.

CARIE AND JACKIE, the two Wisco teammates, were talking it over at Tommy's Lunch in Harvard Square. It was their usual place to have breakfast after morning practice. A couple of the other women were with them, and the rest of the team had gone off to other restaurants. Nancy Storrs, another starboard from the EDC group, always drove a few women out to the International House of Pancakes in Brighton, where they usually had a two-for-one breakfast deal; Claudia Schneider, the quiet California rower, went with some others to a place called Zum-Zums, where they served a particularly delectable jelly. Eating was one of the most enjoyable activities of their day; meals were often long and lingering.

Carie had the same thing for breakfast every morning: a toasted bagel with cream cheese and a lime rickey. The lime rickey was a local drink that she'd developed a taste for, made from lime juice, soda water, and sugar. In bars, it was served with a splash of gin, but no one drank while they were in training. Carie had brought her mail over from Eliot House that morning, and sat reading it aloud to some of the other women in the group who hadn't been fortunate enough to get any. Apparently, the women's coxswain and the men's coxswain from Wisconsin Crew had gotten married, and the coach had been so excited during the service that he had literally jumped up and down.

With the rigid regimen of camp life—the eat, sleep, and row cycle, twice a day, six times a week—most of the women felt like they were stuck out on a ship at sea or on an isolated military base somewhere. The lack of TVs or radios made the daily mail an important link to the real world. But after Carie's letter was read, the discussion quickly fell back to rowing, the morning's practice, and Maggie MacLean.

"It's her own fault," Jackie explained. "She should have known what she was capable of, she should have worn gloves or something. And you don't go crying to the coach or any of that stuff either. I mean, you can't go crying to the coach saying, 'I have my period today and I don't feel well.' I could have done that, I have my period today. But you don't, you just go out there."

"Really," Carie agreed. "You just can't have sympathy for that sort of thing. This is the big time, and you have to know what you're doing. You either make it or break it."

Carie often stuck up for Jackie, who had a tendency to speak her mind rather bluntly. Once, after the Nationals, when they both met Maggie MacLean for the first time, Jackie had made the bold repartee: "Oh, so *you're* Maggie MacLean. Well, I want you to stay away from Mike Vespoli." Vespoli was a member of the U.S. men's eight, and he and Jackie saw each other occasionally. Crew romances, however, could change from week to week, and you had to keep a watchful eye on things.

The two Wisconsin teammates were close and had already been through a lot together. Even though they'd won the Nationals at Princeton and were unmistakably two of the strongest rowers at the camp, they'd had to deal with the superior attitudes of the East Coast rowers, who initially thought of them as a couple of hicks. Sometimes they were referred to as "the cheerleaders," and once, another one of the port recruits had said about Jackie, "I'm certainly not going to lose a seat race to some home economics major from Wisconsin."

Carie and Jackie often kept to themselves and retaliated by talking tough. Now it was time for the final round of cuts, and both women knew that they were probably going to make the boat—it was just a question of whether they would actually row or be a spare. But that morning's practice had been a final reckoning for Maggie, and everyone in the crew knew it.

THE DAY HAD BEGUN gray and drizzly, a temporary break in the hot swelter of late July. The eleven remaining women had gathered briefly on the Newell dock, facing Parker and the river behind him. Harry had made a few dry jokes and then gotten right to the serious business at hand. As soon as he called out the boatings, everyone knew what was up. Two boats of four meant that someone was going to be seat raced.

In seat racing, the eight was broken up into two groups of four and the two people who were being tested against one another sat in the identical seat in opposite boats. A set number of short races, or pieces, were done. Then the boats were brought in and the two people traded boats, to give each person a chance to row in each crew. One of the boats might be inherently faster, despite the efforts of the rower being tested. The boats raced again. The results of each race were recorded.

The seat-racing method may have seemed like a relatively easy way to weed out the weaker rowers, but there were numerous other variables that could confuse the selection process. These either had to be held constant or be taken into consideration by the coach. First, it helped if the boats were relatively equal in speed, so that the racing was close and competitive for the two rowers. In an effort to do this, the coach had to select two equal pairings of fours, and have the stroke of each boat hold to the same stroke rating. If one boat sprinted, and the other rowed low and steady, the contest was inherently unfair.

One big assumption in seat racing was that all the other rowers would row each race equally, with the same amount of effort regardless of who was sitting in the boat with them. Some of this, of course, was difficult to control, and a good coach had to keep an eye on everything, not just the two people being raced. The coach had to remember, for example, that the stroke of one boat might have a tendency to start slow and finish strong, or that someone in the bow of one boat had a cold that day.

Wiki Royden, for example, had a devilish streak and tried to get away with things whenever Harry had her stroke one of the fours. Sometimes she'd try to sprint a little off the starting line, to give her boat a lead before Harry caught on and told her to take the rating back down. When this didn't work, she'd wait until her four was passing under a bridge, and then take the rating up again when no one could see. But once Harry knew what to expect from someone, there was very little that they could do to surprise him. Still, Wiki thought it was awfully fun to try.

Just that morning she had goaded him while they were about to start the pieces.

"Hey, coach," she called out, "what does the big 'H' on your megaphone stand for—*Harvard* or *Harry?*" Some guarded laughter came from the rest of the team, and then silence as they waited for Parker's response.

"They're synonymous," Parker had replied, dryly.

Aside from the human element, there were other, more subtle, calculations that had to be entered into the seat-racing mix. The current or wind might be different in each lane. An errant wake might disturb one crew more than another. Parker not only recorded the results of each race—how much each crew won by— but what the conditions were for each crew, if they were, in fact, different. It was because of all these variables that an individual might not truly know if she had beaten another person or not.

The fours shoved off from the dock and headed downstream, warming up as they passed under the series of low bridges that led them toward the city of Boston: Anderson, Weeks, Western Avenue, and finally River Street, where the large Coca-Cola sign flashed the time and temperature: 7:34 A.M., 74 degrees. The boats swung around to begin the first race, in the short stretch of straight water that was known among the rowers as the "powerhouse stretch." The name actually came from the Cambridge power station sitting midway along the 1000-meter reach, but somehow the name conjured up visions of rowing power, of who could row harder through the gauntlet of bridges.

"Hooo . . . ready!" Parker called out through his megaphone. He stood in the bow of the launch like a field general, directing the two crews together for military maneuvers. He held a silver stopwatch to check the stroke ratings, and his ubiquitous yellow notebook was close at hand. On Parker's command, the two fours surged ahead, eager to get on with the morning's work.

Usually Carie Graves stroked one of the boats, and Anne Warner stroked another. Even when the rivals from Wisconsin and Yale weren't seat racing one another, it seemed like they had begun their own private rivalry to establish who was the superior stroke. Sometimes, even when they were just paddling back to the dock, Carie Graves would make sure her boat got there first, picking up the rating and the power to do so. When Anne tried to call her on this unnecessary competitiveness, Carie explained that her butt hurt when she rowed too slowly, and it simply felt better to paddle in a little faster. Anne just shook her head in reply.

Then there was the other Yalie, Chris Ernst, who kept on winning her seat races against much bigger opponents. Parker had kept on seat racing her against Gail Ricketson and Maggie MacLean, despite the fact that she won every time. Finally, she'd had enough. After beating her larger opponents for yet another time, she cried out to Parker, half in anguish, half in anger,

"WHY DO YOU KEEP DOING THIS TO ME?!"

Harry held out his hand and patted the air in front of him, as if to still it and calm her down at the same time.

But seat racing not only tested the physical resolve of the participants, it measured what Steve Gladstone called "their physical and emotional durability." Sure, a rower might have one good day, but how did they perform over the long haul? Parker didn't have much time to gauge this group of young recruits; he had to put them through some serious, repeated tests, right in the middle of a hot Boston summer.

This morning it was Maggie MacLean against Chris Ernst again; Anne Warner against Jackie Zoch. The results were not very difficult to read and there were no outbursts this time around. Rowing in the slower of the two fours, Anne barely lost the first piece, but won the second by a clear margin. Maggie lost both of her races to Chris.

Everyone knew that Maggie had been beaten, including Maggie herself. Back at the boathouse, after they'd put the eight back on its rack, she stole away to a dark, empty corner of the bays and unwrapped her hands, trying to hide the pain. Then she walked back to the Eliot House dorm with Nancy Storrs in silence. Nancy knew, too.

That afternoon, while the rest of the women were napping, Parker came by and knocked on her door, despite the "Do not disturb" sign hung on it. He tried to explain the situation to her, but Maggie was still in a state of disbelief. By his mere presence, she knew that Harry wanted her in the boat, but now there was simply no way for him to justify it. Later, when she'd had some time to dwell on it, Maggie realized she bore no personal grudge against Harry Parker or anyone.

Something, however, hadn't gone right. For all the merits of the camp system, it had pitted the women against each other in a way that she thought was unfortunate and destructive. Perhaps the new camp system would indeed yield a fast boat, but something unique to crew had been lost—the idea of bringing a group of like-minded souls together and welding them into a tight-knit group who really trusted one other.

On one of the seat races, it seemed like her boat had been far ahead for a while. Then suddenly the power in the four just died, as if one of the women rowing with her had just given up. She knew she hadn't stopped pulling hard. Who was in her boat when that happened? *Wiki . . . Gail Ricketson . . . Jackie Zoch.* Was it possible someone had sandbagged the race?

If so, it was a mean trick, just like the one Jackie Zoch had played on her only a few weeks earlier. Jackie had asked her out to the movies, and they had walked into Harvard Square to the subway stop together. But when the train pulled up and Maggie stepped on, she turned around and saw Jackie still standing on the platform.

"C'mon," Maggie said. "What are you waiting for?"

"I've———decided not to go," said Jackie.

Before Maggie could fathom the reason for Jackie's behavior, the subway doors suddenly closed between them and the train began to move away. Mystified, she headed off to the movies alone, and it wasn't until the next day that she discovered the real reason she'd been ditched.

That same night Mike Vespoli had come to town.

AT FIVE O'CLOCK, the women reassembled for the afternoon practice and Maggie MacLean was not among them. Parker stood waiting for the pre-practice banter to subside, then made his announcement in a low, serious voice:

"I've . . . spoken to Maggie, and I . . . told her she won't be with us."

He looked around at the group, trying to gauge the reaction. A small smile escaped from his lips.

"I guess now I can congratulate you all, and I guess now you can relax a little too. I'm sorry this past week has been quite as full of tension as it has. I just . . . wanted to give Maggie a chance to see if she was capable of helping us."

Everyone was quiet, partly relieved, but still uncertain as to the final seating of the crew. One person had been eliminated, but there were still ten rowers assembled on the dock for eight seats.

"Now I guess the question is when the boat will be settled," Parker continued, correctly reading everyone's thoughts. "I guess the question I have for you is whether you'll be comfortable with having not eight people settled, but having ten of you all capable, and at some time I'll tell you what I think will be the best setup."

Again Parker paused, gauging the effect of his words. He knew they could not be happy about this decision, but it was the only way to keep everyone striving to do better now that the main selection process was over. The group couldn't afford to sit back and be comfortable now, to feel like they owned their seats.

A low groan issued from the group.

"If that proves to be too unnerving, I'd be willing to settle it. But that's my inclination right now. There'll be no more seat racing for a while, but we might want to look at a question or two." Another wry smile crossed his lips. At this, a few more groans and hisses issued from the group, followed by a burst of laughter. If the seat racing had indeed been a cruel version of musical chairs, now Harry was basically telling them that the music hadn't quite stopped playing.

Carie Graves, sitting down on the dock in front of Parker, suddenly started squirming uncontrollably. "*I think a spider just crawled up my pants!*" she said. More laughter came from the ten rowers, and finally the tension that had hung in the air all day was broken. Lynn Silliman grabbed a water bottle and started squirting Carie with it. Chris Ernst restarted her running commentary from the bow seat as all hands got on the eight and hoisted it aloft to bring it down to the water. Ernst could barely reach the gunwales when the boat was briefly held overhead, but when it was brought down to shoulder level, she was fine.

At least for the moment, Chris Ernst had made it. And as she emerged from the dark bays of Newell and out onto the sunny dock, bearing the boat on her shoulder, somehow the boathouse and the camp were not so intimidating anymore. Then she was sitting in the bow of the eight, tying into the shoes—a part of something she had truly earned. Chris Ernst had proven herself on the water, where everything really mattered.

Suddenly, from somewhere, a Frisbee went flying. Nancy Storrs caught it from the three seat and threw it back. Then the eight shoved off and moved away from the dock, the chosen rowers filled with a renewed burst of energy. The boat shot away like an arrow, full of purpose and direction. After a short practice, they returned to Newell and fooled around some more, happy to have made the final cut. Then Nancy Storrs brought out a cake with mocha icing and candles on it, even though it was no one's birthday.

"What's the occasion?" someone asked, as everyone gathered around the cake.

"The occasion," Nancy Storrs announced, "is that we are now going to have to get along with one another!"

"Don't we already," someone shouted, "even if we hate each other?"

Eleven

THIS WAS JUST THE SORT OF SITUATION that Gail Pierson had always dreaded. Perhaps the seat racing had sifted out the weaker rowers, but it was much too cutthroat and had turned them into a bunch of pirates—not a real crew that respected each other. Somehow, they had to move away from the infighting and begin to treat themselves as a team. But even at the start of the next week, when they were back in the eight again, a small conspiracy had begun against Carie Graves. A few rowers had apparently gone to Harry behind her back and questioned her ability to continue as stroke. Carie, they told him, was staying out quite late, sometimes not even returning to the Harvard dorms.

Apparently, Carie Graves had found a new boyfriend.

ARTHUR GRACE was a free-lance photographer living in Cambridge that summer. A New Englander who spent most of his time, in Massachusetts, he had nevertheless led an unusual life coming of age in the '60s. He was the New England correspondent for *The*

New York Times, and his free-lance work often took him to strange places, to cover stories for magazines like *Time* and *People*. Little did he know that one of his most intriguing stories would take place right in the middle of Cambridge.

He'd never covered women's sports before, although he'd shot Caroline Kennedy playing field hockey once at Radcliffe. He wasn't even a sports photographer, although he'd covered a few men's tennis matches and a few Patriots games. When he arrived at the Harvard Boathouse, he was taken aback by the scene in front of him: a bunch of big, strong women who so deftly managed a sixty-foot-long boat. He felt like he'd entered a world inhabited by Amazons.

He'd seen strong women before, in the U.S. Marines and at a kibbutz in Israel; he knew that women were capable of hard physical labor. But this was different. These women *chose* to be here, *chose* to subject themselves to a physical challenge that most men would shy away from. Sure, there were individual women out there who were amazing athletes: Peggy Fleming in skating, Billie Jean King in tennis. But crew seemed to have a brutal, macho aspect to it. He'd never seen any teams of women who could do what this group could do, to push themselves to the very limits of their being in order to propel a narrow boat up and down the river.

He thought it was somewhat bizarre at first, then he realized that it was actually quite beautiful. In crew the rowers' bodies became secondary, lost in the synchronous movement of the oars and the smooth movement of the shell itself. Perhaps on dry land, these women didn't fit the traditional definition of feminine beauty, being either too big or too muscular. But when they took to the water, they became transformed, part of a giant swan with eight wings. It was a powerful image to behold, and one that he wanted to capture on film.

At first, he was too busy at his work to notice anyone in particular. Every photo shoot has its own set of challenges, and the water and the fast movement of the rowers made this one no exception. He leaned out over bridges, knelt down on the dock, and rode around in the launch with Parker, trying to get the perfect shot without interfering with the crew practice. Because of the length of the boat and the fact that all the rowers faced backwards, he soon found himself shooting the team from various angles just off their stern. This was the classic crew shot, the only way to capture all eight rowers without using a wide-angle lens. Still, even this shot had its deficits. You only showed the back of the coxswain this way, and you always focused on one rower—the stroke.

Carie Graves appeared in his lens so often that he couldn't help but be drawn to her. She was clearly the leader, the biggest one in the boat, and in Arthur's eyes the most attractive. He'd never gotten involved with a subject before, but before he realized what was happening, he was following her over Anderson Bridge after practice, asking her if she wanted to see some of his work.

Despite the difference in their ages and backgrounds, the two soon discovered they had a lot in common. Carie was flattered by the attention of the older man, who'd traveled around the world as much as she had. He too was a free spirit, much more sophisticated than any of the Wisconsin boys she'd met, including her current boyfriend, Ira. Arthur had been to a kibbutz, as she had, had dropped out of college and gone to California for a year, where he learned how to surf. Before she knew it, she had moved out of the dorms at Eliot House and into his apartment on Franklin Street. She wrote a note to Ira and told him that it was over between them.

The move out of the Eliot House dorms and into Arthur's world provided Carie with some relief from the monotony of camp life. When he wasn't off on assignment, working long, odd hours, Arthur hung out with a bohemian crowd, who would much rather smoke cigarettes and listen to music than push themselves to the brink of physical collapse. Part of Carie had always been drawn to that sort of lifestyle, and it reminded her that life did exist outside of rowing.

One of Arthur's best friends was a guy appropriately named Buzzy, who managed various rock bands around New England, including groups like The Animals. When Buzzy met Carie, he could barely contain his shock. He acted like Arthur had brought home some strange new creature. He had never seen a woman of her size and stature.

How strong was she? Buzzy wondered.

Carie proposed that they have a leg-wrestling match to settle the matter immediately. Before he could object, Buzzy was lying down butt-to-butt with a mad, leg-wrestling woman from Wisconsin. Carie had already leg-wrestled Arthur and beaten him, despite the fact that he had a muscular, athletic build. Buzzy didn't stand a chance. When his scrawny leg connected with Carie's, he was instantly thrown backwards across the floor of Arthur's apartment. Their introduction settled, the two became good friends. Sometimes Buzzy would invite Carie to listen to his bands play when they were practicing or recording an album.

The music and the mixed company took Carie's mind off the stresses of her training schedule, and she was happy to have moved off the Harvard campus. Some of her teammates, however, didn't see it in such a positive light. They saw it as a symbolic defection from the camp. And so they had approached Harry Parker and told him about it. Whether they were genuinely worried about her well-being, or just jealous that she had a boyfriend, was unclear. But apparently Harry had promised to look into it, however tactfully he could, for after one particularly grueling workout of three three-mile pieces, he slowly approached the crew in his red launch and asked Carie how she felt. It was a weird question for someone like Parker to ask.

"Tired," she replied, looking a little confused. "Isn't that how I'm *supposed* to feel?"

It wasn't until a few weeks later that Carie caught wind of the conspiracy and finally figured out Parker's remarks. She was angry that anyone would question how she conducted herself outside the boat. Perhaps the women who had spoken to Parker felt that she had broken the implicit training rules of abstinence in crew. Most oarsmen in serious training didn't drink alcohol, and some even subscribed to the notion that sex sapped one's physical energy. Realistically, Carie knew that most of them were simply too tired to have a social life outside of crew.

As for her, she could stay up all night with Arthur and still beat any one of them in a seat race. Whoever they were, they had no right poking their noses into her private life and relaying it to Parker. After all, Gail Pierson practically lived with her boyfriend, Sy Cromwell, and no one called her night life into question. What were they supposed to be anyway, a bunch of Catholic schoolgirls?

Arthur had his own theory about the conspiracy: he thought a few of the women on the team were simply jealous. He didn't worry that the affair would affect Carie's performance, for he sensed right away that the woman he'd fallen in love with had a passion for rowing that no man would ever extinguish. Part of his attraction to Carie was, in fact, that she was so driven to fulfill her goal as an athlete. It was a passion that matched his own drive to succeed as a photojournalist. A man could put his passion in two places, why couldn't a woman? He also had enough sense to realize that a man or a woman in love actually had more energy than one who was not.

Parker wasn't someone to take an interest in matters outside the boat and never brought the issue up again. If Carie had enough drive to devote herself to rowing twice a day and having a boyfriend at night, that was her business. Parker himself had a wife and two children, and still managed to do all that he did without much trouble. The matter settled, it was time to move beyond the personal squabbles within the boat and focus on what still lay ahead.

NOW THAT THE EIGHT WAS CHOSEN, more or less, it was time to start proving themselves as a real crew, to get away from the infighting and do what they were being trained to do. There wasn't much time before they'd have to test themselves against the rest of the world. Unfortunately, on the Charles River there was little competition for them. The river was largely vacant of crews in the summertime with all the colleges out of session.

Canadian Henley, an annual mid-summer's race held in St. Catherine's, Ontario, provided the first real challenge for the ten women. Harry raced them in an eight, as well as two fours. This allowed him to see a little more clearly which cluster of rowers performed better in competition and to observe how the eight rowed against some other fast women's boats. Although none of the world contenders were there, the results were very optimistic. The eight easily handled the best Canadian clubs, from which an Olympic eight would emerge in '76. Now at least they knew they were the fastest crew of eight women in North America.

In the fours, the grouping of Carie Graves, Gail Pierson, Claudia Schneider, and Carol Brown easily outrowed the other four of Anne Warner, Gail Ricketson, Jackie Zoch, and Chris Ernst. Breaking the eight into fours allowed Parker to sneak in one last seat race, a way to reconfirm a few of his choices. Ricketson and Zoch remained the spares for now.

Aside from determining how strong or effective an individual rower was, racing in fours had the additional benefit of helping a coach identify combinations of rowers who rowed well together. Some of this had already come out in the seat-racing process, but some of it could only emerge through practice in the eight itself. And this was his main focus now, to finalize the seating plan of the big boat.

In a way, this part of Parker's job was similar to a photographer's. The composition of a crew was like the composition of a good photo: it had to have both balance and clarity. This required an excellent eye for detail, of knowing each rower's individual style and ability, in order to place them well in relation to the rest of the crew.

The orchestration of the rowers ideally had to be done as unobtrusively as possible, in order to facilitate the more organic process that happened by simply letting the crew row together over time. A coach who meddled too much was like a photographer who was constantly trying to move his subjects around—telling them not only where but how to hold their bodies, mussing with their hair and other aspects of their appearance. In rowing, this made the oarsmen feel too self-conscious and singled out, distracting their focus from the rest of the crew.

There were different theories about how to arrange a crew. A coach could, for example, select a boat based purely on power, putting the strongest people in the stern seats of the boat and letting the weaker rowers follow. That wasn't a bad general plan, but it didn't account for the fact that some rowers, often the more aggressive ones, weren't always the easiest ones to follow. They might not have a consistent sense of rhythm, which made it difficult for those seated behind them.

A boat could also be organized based on efficiency of technique, placing the more graceful rowers in the stern seats and letting the "hammers" follow. This plan, too, had merit, but it had some obvious deficiencies as well. A boat couldn't be led by those who were purely technicians. There had to be a certain amount of aggressiveness in the lead seats in order to provide the spark for the crew. Thus, it was a much greater challenge than one might think to identify and distribute the rowers based on their power, technique, and personality.

Some thought there was a specific recipe for a good crew, based on the different qualities of each seat. But a boat could not be so easily typecast. In reality, the coach kept trying different combinations, shuffling the deck until the right cards fell into place for a royal flush.

Clearly, as even Arthur Grace had guessed, the stroke was the most important seat of the boat, if any one seat held more importance than another. It was the heart of the crew, the pacemaker. Without a good stroke, the boat couldn't function properly, couldn't find an effective rhythm to sustain both its speed and endurance. Parker often built his crews around this seat, choosing the person who had the right amount of aggressiveness tempered by a sense of rhythm.

A good stroke had the tenacity of a pit bull. More than this, however, the stroke was someone the others could follow and put their entire confidence in. Despite the laments about her late night behavior, no one ever doubted that this seat would be given to Carie—except perhaps Anne Warner. As Anne knew from stroking the Yale varsity, Carie was an odd choice for the lead seat. She was powerful and aggressive, but certainly not always the easiest person to follow.

Behind Carie he had placed the two scullers, Gail Pierson and Wiki Royden. A seven-seat oar also needed to be one of the best technicians in the crew, but didn't need the absolute and almost self-righteous certainty of the stroke. What the seven seat needed was the same sense of rhythm as the stroke, but also the capacity to follow exactly the movements of the leader. If a good stroke rowed with an intuitive sense of pacing and power, a good seven seat did so through more calculated, thoughtful means. Perhaps it was the calculating, analytic part of her nature that prevented Gail from being the right choice for stroke, but made her the right choice for the seat right behind Carie. The only problem with Gail, however, was that she was sometimes late at the catch, not a good thing for the starboards behind her to follow.

The stroke and the seven seat, taken together, were a sub-unit known as the stern pair. When a coach was looking for combinations of people who rowed well together, this pairing was one of the most critical in the boat. The port side all took their timing from the stroke's oar; the starboards took theirs from the seven seat.

Thus, if there was no synergy between the stroke and the seven seat, the boat would not function smoothly, with the starboard side slightly out of synch with the ports. But somehow, even with Gail's occasional off-placed catches, the boat seemed to operate well.

Behind Gail, Parker placed Wiki Royden, the other sculler and former Radcliffe stroke. With a top-notch sculler, a coach knew he was getting someone who rowed well and could push herself to her limits. Gail and Wiki were both accomplished in the single and didn't require the external incentive of other rowers. They already knew how to get the most out of every stroke. The only problem with both of them was that, as scullers, they had a tendency to look out of the boat. This was acceptable in a single, to see where you were going, but a cardinal sin in team rowing.

The middle four seats of the boat, the six through the three seat, were commonly known as the "engine room," the section that held the biggest, most powerful athletes. In terms of boat physics, it was good to distribute the greatest weight here, so that the hull would ride evenly in the water as it was designed to do.

The engine room rowers needed good power and length through the water. They might not be as technically adept or as aggressive as the stern pair, but they generally had more raw power. The five seat sat in the exact center of the boat and was usually occupied by a big, strong rower. Maggie MacLean had always rowed the five seat, and in the middle of an eight, her weight and rough stroke had not been an issue. But in a four during seat races, it had perhaps proved her undoing.

Claudia Schneider now filled the spot. At Canadian Henley, she had proven her true value and discovered a fighting streak that had been well hidden within her. From the five seat, she also saw herself as the link between the bow and the stern, the one who could bring the three women ahead of her into alignment. She didn't watch Gail's or Carie's oar specifically; instead she looked forward and tried to take it all in—the swinging of the bodies, the placement of the blades.

Anne Warner, at four, found herself doing much the same thing, trying to make sense of the mild chaos presented by Carie, Gail, and Wiki. It had been difficult for her not to be the stroke, and she had even talked briefly with Harry about it. Technically, she could row better than some of the people in front of her. Why then was she sitting behind them now?

Privately, Parker reassured her. "Don't worry so much about what seat you end up in. Every seat makes a contribution to the whole."

He had first tried Anne at six. She was, after all, a little bigger than Wiki, but she seemed to have problems following Carie's stroke—perhaps because of the competitiveness between them. And so she ended up in the four seat, the leader of the "bow four" of the boat—another cluster including the four, three, two, and bow seats. That was why when they broke up into fours to race at Canadian Henley, she had been the stroke of the second boat.

That at least was a small consolation, even if she couldn't yet understand Harry's seating plan.

The three seat, where Nancy Storrs had been placed, was sometimes jokingly described as the position you stuck the starboard rower who didn't fit anywhere else. Three-seat oarsmen were generally "hammers"—they had good power but weren't technically adept enough to row at either end of the boat. Their strokes might be a little choppy or short, or perhaps they didn't have quite enough flexibility. But they sure knew how to move an oar through the water.

The stroke and the seven seat had their understudies in the two and bow seats. If it was challenging to row in the lead seats of the boat, it was perhaps equally challenging to row in the last two seats, where you had to follow everyone else.

The bow was where the boat pitched around the most, making it more difficult to get your oar in and out of the water cleanly. It required great finesse and quickness, and often this meant a smaller rower whose stroke might be shorter, but whose reflexes were faster than anyone else's. If the bow pair didn't do their job well, the balance of the boat would deteriorate in rough water. Many novice coaches put the weakest two rowers in the bow, and their boats suffered because of it. A wise coach knew the importance of placing technically sharp rowers at both ends of the boat.

Carol Brown and Chris Ernst were perfect as the bow pair.

Brown, whom Parker had placed in the two seat, usually rowed six in the Princeton varsity. For a while at the camp, she'd been placed at six, but then she'd been shifted back to last port seat, displaced by Wiki Royden. At Princeton, she was one of the bigger, stronger rowers. Among this group, however, she was one of the smallest, not much bigger than Chris Ernst. She knew she had made this boat on the basis of her rowing merit and her cardiovascular ability. Like Wiki, she'd also been a competitive swimmer and often wore wildly colored Speedo swimsuits to crew practice. Beneath two long braids in which she gathered her hair were a well-developed set of shoulders and arms. And she had refined her rowing skills in the pair at the 1974 World Championships.

A pair was the smallest form of sweep boat and the most difficult to master. Because there were only two rowers in it, each holding one oar, any discrepancies in technique or power between the two would immediately cause a problem with the boat's balance. Perhaps even more so than single sculling, the mastery of a pair gave a rower superior ability to hold down the center of balance in the boat and deal with the pitching when things got rough.

Temperamentally as well, Brown was well suited for the two seat. While she'd been a leader back at Princeton, the captain of both the swim team and the crew team, most of what she did was behind the scenes. She spent a lot of her time and energy getting these programs up and running, often sacrificing her own individual potential. After her success in the pair at the 1974 World Championships, she could have easily abandoned her Princeton squad and focused on her own rowing career, as Wiki had done in the single scull. Instead she returned and gained more ground for the women's team, impressing the Princeton coaches with her performance and helping the women gain more access to the boathouse.

So finally Parker had his crew pretty well sorted out. And it was a very odd-looking boat indeed. They were as different from one another as some of the outfits they wore: Carie Graves with her headband and big hoop earrings, Gail Pierson with her Carhart duck-hunting cap, Carol Brown with her psychedelic Speedo swimsuits and long Indian braids, Chris Ernst with her red handkerchief and her wire-rimmed glasses.

And now that his final eight was more or less chosen, he brought them downstream for one final test.

IN ORDER TO SECURE FUNDING for their trip to England, the crew had to break a time standard set by the NRF to prove that they could be competitive with the rest of the world-class field. The Olympic funds that Gail Pierson had finally secured for the team wouldn't kick in until the following year, and the NRF officials weren't going to send any more women's boats across the Atlantic only to have them come back home with their tails between their legs. The team certainly couldn't afford to send themselves. On the way back from Canadian Henley, they'd had to break into the Syracuse boathouse to spend the night because none of them had enough money for a hotel room.

Harry had estimated that the total cost for each of his athletes to go to the Nottingham World Championships would be about $783.86. This included their airfare to London; room and board at Henley, where they would train for ten days; and room and board for a week at Nottingham itself. The Olympic Committee could only give them a hundred dollars per athlete to offset these expenses, but the NRF had agreed to pay $577.50 per athlete—*if* they made the time standard. The Olympic money and the NRF contribution would reduce their expenses to a mere $106.36.

The time they had to break was 3:18 over 1000 meters. They

had only pulled a 3:22 up in Canada, but the 101-degree heat had been so intense that thirty-two entrants had scratched. Parker had made his picks, more or less, and the boat felt fast—very fast. For all their different personalities, everybody sensed this. They had never been part of such a dynamic crew—one that would row hard whether there was a competitor next to them or not. For all his reserve, even Parker had recently admitted to a *Boston Globe* reporter that this was indeed the fastest U.S. women's boat he'd ever seen. That had finally pricked up the ears of the press. The *Globe* had run a special feature on the boat and called it "Harry's 'other' crew." Now some of the burden to perform well rested on his shoulders.

The eight had an intrinsic energy to it, despite the strong individuals who sat in the boat and sometimes clearly disliked each other outside of it. This ran counter to the ideal notion of crew, the one that was sometimes served up as the model for corporate success. In a good crew, it was said, everyone got along and worked together to achieve a common goal. But in reality, as Parker knew, this wasn't always true.

What the women did have to do was put their differences aside and focus on one thing, making the eight go fast. When the boat was moving well, it was easy to do this, to tap into something more powerful and important than oneself by getting lost in the shared, repeated motion of the other rowers. And once the boat went to full pressure, there was really no other option. This is what crew intrinsically offered that other team sports could only seldom achieve—rowing hard *obliterated* individual egos.

In a sport like baseball, for a team to shine, each player had to do their specific job well. Everyone had a different task. But in rowing, the different numbers on the seats became superfluous when a crew was really rowing well. There was no other team sport, in fact, in which the movements of eight individuals had to be so perfectly matched to one another. A crew was an eight-cylinder racing machine, where all the cylinders fired at once. A crew coach was the mechanic, building up the engine from scratch and then testing it again and again, to make certain it would work.

More often than not, Parker's crews won. The names of the Harvard boys changed from year to year, but their success was pretty much a constant, almost a given. The past two seasons had been no exception; in fact, the crews of '74 and '75 epitomized all that a Parker-coached Harvard crew was. The nickname for the '74 boat had been the "Rude and Smooth," and it contained some of the best varsity oarsmen ever to walk through Newell. They were so good, in fact, that years later, Parker hung an action shot of the crew in the entryway of the men's boathouse.

It was a photo of the crew at full tilt, pulling at the oars as hard as they could. The shot captured what was rarely noticed in crew racing: the absolute frenzy, or wildness, of a boat fully engaged in battle. Unlike what people saw from a distance—the graceful movement of the oars and the boat—it was not a pretty sight. The individuals of the crew almost seemed at odds with each other—some leaning out to port, some to starboard, some even looking out of the boat.

From the photo at least, the "Rude and Smooth" looked like it had no sense of poise or group unity whatsoever. What was very apparent, however, from looking at the faces in the boat, was that Parker had put together a crew of oarsmen with the killer instinct.

And now this strange women's crew, he had begun to realize, was going to have a rude and smooth legacy of their own. But before they could prove that to the rest of the world, they would have to prove it to themselves and the stopwatch.

THE BASIN was where the Charles River spread out like a large open lake, created by the dam restricting the river's flow into Boston Harbor. It was a beautiful body of water that shimmered in the early morning light, with the sun rising up behind the Boston cityscape and casting even its tallest buildings in shadow. On the river in the early morning these appeared two-dimensional, like part of a backdrop for an old movie.

Much of the view on this part of the Charles was in fact a grand illusion, the creation of a powerful group of Harvard alumni who had changed a virtual mud flat into a huge water park. Before the dam had been put in, separating the river from Boston Harbor, the Charles had been a tidal waterway, rising and falling nearly ten feet with the tides. It was an ugly sight, especially at low tide, when the river was reduced to a trickle and the swampy banks were fully exposed. Finally, enough people complained about it and a plan was proposed to turn the eyesore into a watery paradise.

Some of the men who had been responsible for the transformation were not only Harvard alumni, but former oarsmen. James Storrow, after whom Storrow Drive was named, had been the captain of the 1885 Harvard crew and was a major force behind the creation of the dam. A powerful banker, he claimed to be obsessed with the idea of making the Charles a place of beauty for all of Boston to enjoy, regardless of social status. Henry Lee Higginson, another Harvard alum, became his partner in the effort. Higginson had been responsible for the creation of the Boston Symphony Orchestra, and he wielded considerable political influence. Rumor had it, however, that the damming of the river and creation of the basin was simply a secret Harvard plot to provide a better rowing course for its crew.

Whatever the real motivation was, the rowers were definitely the major beneficiaries of the project, inheriting a sparkling jewel in the heart of Boston that most of its residents never experienced firsthand. They never knew what it was like to see their city from the inside out, from an oasis of natural calm and beauty.

To a crew coach out practicing with his team, only the river really mattered. The city surrounding it disappeared, and the water alone seemed real and alive. Despite the dam, you could often smell a saltiness in the air, reminding you that on the other side of the tall buildings lay the harbor, and beyond that the Atlantic Ocean. There were a *few* moments, usually toward the end of a crew season, when the romantic notions of being out on the river actually held true, when you noticed how beautiful the river really was, with all its natural grandeur and man-made history. This was usually a point late in the season when the main bulk of the work was over, and your crews had done well (or hadn't), and the racing season was suddenly and quickly coming to an end. By then a coach like Parker had looked at his crew enough times to know that he had done everything he could do, that they would win or not win. At this point a coach began to move away from the crew, to let them find their own sense of rhythm and speed. Hopefully at this point the rowers had turned further within themselves, searching for their own source of power.

The women would begin the timed piece well upstream from the dam, near the Mass. Avenue bridge. An NAAO official sat in Harry's launch, stopwatch in hand, waiting for them to line up and get ready. It was the middle of the summer and it was quite hot. The surface of the Charles River had a flat, sleepy quality to it that was broken only by the occasional wake of a pleasure boat making its way downstream. It felt odd to be rowing a race alone, without the benefit of another boat beside them, but in theory, this was what good rowing was really all about—testing the limits within your own crew. In practice, however, rowing alone against the clock was a difficult proposition.

This kind of race required a group of individuals who were intensely self-motivated, who didn't need other boats around to go as hard as they could go. In this respect, Parker had chosen the right crew, for almost everyone sitting in the boat was on a personal quest for something that went well beyond rowing. For some, like Gail Pierson, this timed piece was part of a long, political journey, helping women to prove themselves as true athletes. For her, it was history in the making—or not. For others, like Carie Graves, it was an internal battle against her own personal demons.

But whatever the different sources of motivation were, they needed to be pooled together now and used as collective fuel for the crew.

They began the piece on Parker's command. They knew what they had to do, but weren't quite sure if they knew how to do it.

For a group that had battled against each other all summer and had barely sat in the same lineup for more than a few days, the idea of coming together had gotten a little lost. But it was something they had to start relearning, and quickly. Otherwise the whole concept of the national team camp would be called into question, the idea that eight strangers could come together as a fast boat. Not only that, but their individual rowing odysseys would end right here in Boston, where no one was watching and nobody really cared.

If they shared one thing, it was a love for the sense of speed and power that came through rowing. There was nothing, simply nothing, like a fast boat. As the eight did their start and came quickly up to speed, it was only moving at about ten miles an hour, but because the rowers were sitting right on top of the water, it appeared to be rushing by them much faster. With each stroke, their bodies surged toward the bow with a powerful push of the legs that nearly lifted them off their sliding seats. They sent the boat forward with a quick, strong pulse, forcing Lynn Silliman to brace herself lightly and hold the gunnels, so as not to be jerked backward with each catch. It was the movement of the rowers' bodies, traveling back and forth, that really contributed to the sense of speed and exhilaration that made rowing almost feel like flying. And as the boat picked up more and more speed, the bodies moved faster, creating a snowball effect that was both intense and hypnotic.

This boat, they all knew, was the fastest any of them had been in. And that realization made them pull even harder.

They'd begun the 1000 meters at the Harvard Bridge, the longest span across the Charles River. It connected Back Bay to

Kendall Square, where MIT had migrated during the 1940s. Just off to port was the neon Citgo sign that stood over the left field wall of Fenway Park, where at night you could see the stadium lights and sometimes hear the Boston fans screaming and blowing horns. But as they rowed by and finished with a final ten, they heard and saw nothing. And afterward, when they sat idle, there was only silence, only the gentle lapping of the waves against the hull as the women waited to hear the results.

Gail Pierson looked over at Parker, conferring with the NAAO official, and thought she detected a smile break across his stony face. That smile was worth a thousand screaming fans, for it meant that together they'd just made it, just hit their own home run, eight bats swinging together with such power that their spirits were lifted high over the confines of the Charles and Boston and even the country itself.

Harry Parker and his pirate crew were heading overseas to England.

AMERICANS ABROAD

T w e l v e

THE IMPERIAL HOTEL had originally been built in
1897, and when the American women arrived in the village of Henley it still possessed some of its eclectic,
Edwardian charm. The entryway looked like something from the
arts and crafts movement, with gold-lettered script set onto a
black iron trellis. Inside, the foyer floor was set with tiny Roman
tiles and opened into a small dining room with a high ceiling and
beautiful rose-colored windows.

On the outside, the facade was white stucco and dark oak, broken up by a band of brickwork and lines of tall windows divided
into small square lights. Between the first and second floor, two
large, horizontal oak panels were set into the house, carved with a
Celtic design of the "green man"—a Pan-like figure whose legs
never ended, just trailed off into curling roots connected to other
animistic figures of the forest. Two imposing chimneys rose from
the side of the dormered roof, and a terra cotta dragon looked
down from its perch on the main ridge beam.

It had a magical, fairy tale feel to it that suited the temperament of the American oarswomen. In short order, they had taken

over the entire third floor and felt comfortable enough to hang their sweaty workout clothing from the louvered windows on the front of the building. But the appearance of Carol Brown's bra one morning, waved like a flag and then tossed down to the cobblestone streets below, may have caused some of the conservative residents of Henley to wonder if the Imperial had become a house of ill repute.

It was, in any case, a great improvement from the first place that Parker had booked them into, some rooms above a noisy pub known as the Five Horseshoes Hotel.

Every morning at dawn the team would spill out of the elegant doors of the Imperial and onto the sleepy streets of Henley—past the boat rental yard of Hobbs and Sons, Ltd., where a paddle wheel boat named the *New Orleans* lay waiting for its daily ration of tourists, along the cobblestone quay that bordered the River Thames, past the Henley Tea Rooms and the Angel Pub, just across from the tower of St. Mary of the Virgin Church, which overlooked the entire town and was made of shards of flint stone and mortar. Henley had a quaint, museum-like quality to it, despite what it looked like when Harry Parker had been there a month previous with his Harvard boys to race.

At that early hour of the morning, the local fishermen were the only ones awake, returning from an evening spent on the peaceful Thames riverbank. Their encounters with the boisterous band of American women—traipsing down to the water wearing nothing but shorts and tank tops and carrying on the way they often did— drew silent, shocked expressions. The fishermen had never seen such a vision before, a group of scantily clad women flaunting their muscles and mouths as they made their way down to the river. And they had seen plenty of rowers before.

The little village where Harry Parker had brought them was in fact best known for the regatta it hosted every summer. The Henley Royal Regatta was one of the oldest, and certainly the most prestigious, rowing events in the world, and it drew a crowd of international-class oarsmen and well-dressed spectators. It was a grand affair for rowers and non-rowers alike. During Henley Week, between late June and early July, the grassy banks along the upper Thames were lined with women in long summer dresses and broad-brimmed hats, and men in navy blue or brightly colored blazers and white cotton trousers.

The regatta had begun modestly in 1839 as an afternoon affair for local British oarsmen who wished to test their skill against one another. Over the years, however, it had expanded to include foreign crews and scullers, and had extended its length to the current five-day affair. Since 1851, when Prince Albert had become a patron of the event, a member of the royal family had always been on hand to distribute some of the most elegantly wrought prizes an oarsman could ever hope to win: the Diamond Sculls, the Princess Elizabeth Cup, and the Silver Goblets, to name but a few.

Some thought that the involvement of the royals had made Henley into the grand event it had become and had been responsible for extending its popularity well beyond the sphere of rowing enthusiasts. Like Wimbledon, which was often held during the same week, Henley had become part of the British high social calendar, and it possessed an indisputable aristocratic air that made it much more than just an athletic fete. The local innkeepers, however, had another explanation for the crowds. During Henley Week, the blue laws that restricted drinking were relaxed, encouraging a flood of students from Oxford and Cambridge who would come to drink their fill of Brakespears, the local Henley brew.

One of the more popular pubs, the Angel, stood at the foot of the Henley Bridge, which connected the village to the regatta enclosures. Both the pub and the bridge were over 100 years old, and both were flooded with people during regatta week. The Angel pub was a tall, white stone building that stood out like a tollhouse overlooking the River Thames. The little stone bridge was originally a Roman structure, and still paid homage to twin pagan gods. The face of Thamisis, or Father Thames, adorned the center of its downstream side, while the goddess Isis overlooked the upstream reach. The bridge would have fit in well back in Boston, but otherwise very little about the river or the town was even remotely similar to anything the women had ever seen.

Everything in Henley seemed to emanate from the river, as if the town still paid tribute to the waters that gave it birth. Henley was formally known as Henley-on-Thames, and before the construction of paved roads and rails, the river had been the lifeblood between the small village and the city of London. The numerous tow paths and locks along the Thames had allowed the passage of trade goods to flow between the city and the small town. But in the 1840s, Henley had been passed over as a major stop on the new British rail system, the Great Western Railway. As a result, the little town was left to settle into a timeless, unspoiled state.

It was rowing, curiously enough, that had prevented the town from becoming a total backwater.

After they'd passed by the Angel and crossed over the Henley Bridge, the women's team would walk along the high iron gate surrounding the elegant Leander Club. Leander was one of the most prestigious rowing clubs in England and the original sponsor of the Henley Royal Regatta. It was also an exclusive social club, closed to the public and the rowing community in general. Only oarsmen who had won at Henley, in fact, would normally be invited to join and proudly wear the club's unusual colors—a shade of pink referred to as *cerise*.

The British, who had given rowing to the world, certainly knew how to host a regatta. During Henley Week, an entire stretch of riverbank opposite the town, the Berkshire side, would be set up with grandstands, fences, and dressing tents. Everything was cordoned off and cut into various enclosures, each with its own function and formal requirements for entry. Heading downstream from the Leander Club, just past the finish line, was a long row of blue-and-white canvas boat tents, set up side by side and looking like the temporary quarters of a desert caravan. Here the oarsmen and their boats were neatly stored.

Next came the socially desirable Steward's Enclosure, restricted to those with special badges, either procured through membership in Leander or by invitation. The Steward's Enclosure was not only the prime viewing area for the races, just adjacent to the finish line, but also the place to see and be seen. In front of the grandstands was a grassy promenade, where you could watch either the crews or the other spectators, dressed in their semi-formal attire. A strict dress code was in place here. Jackets and ties were required of men, who often sported their school colors and either beanies or straw boaters. Women had to wear hats and dresses cut below the knee.

Behind the grandstands was a food and drink area, where you could take tea and cakes if you had purchased a lunch ticket, or sit at either the Bridge bar or the Fawley and have a glass of Pimms as you swapped old rowing tales. Or, if you tired of both the racing and the conversation, you could listen to the brass orchestra, the Honourable Artillery Company, which played a full program of classical tunes throughout the day. In short, it was an event that had two sides to it, the social and the athletic, and each was to be enjoyed in its proper place and perspective.

The course itself, held on the longest straight stretch of river that could accommodate two crews, was outlined by a series of posts and booms—long wooden beams that were linked together and floated on the surface of the water to help eliminate errant wakes. Elegant umpire launches with names like *Ulysses* and *Empress* followed the crews up and down the course and made sure that no foul play occurred between boats. Along the Buckinghamshire side, adjacent to the town, spectators watched the regatta from private boats, punts, or small wooden rowing skiffs with lapstrake hulls and wicker seats.

Needless to say, Henley was unlike any sporting event that

took place in the United States. It had an atmosphere of traditional pageantry, and with the dress code came a sense of propriety that most Americans might have mistaken for a lack of interest—but the Brits were keen sporting enthusiasts. Although the crowd's reaction was generally held to a titter or a modest roar, they certainly responded to close racing, especially when it came down to the final strokes between a favored foreign crew and one of their own. Otherwise, emotions were muted, in typical British fashion, and in keeping with the overall tenor of the event.

The oarsmen themselves were to be seen on the course, but not milling among the spectators, dressed in their sweaty garb and drawing attention to themselves. Rowers were, in a sense, treated more like actors, and the river was simply the theater where they put on their play. If you were a gentleman, once you finished your race and paddled out of view, you were expected to put away your boat and oars and then quietly rejoin the rest of society, cleaned up and dressed in your jacket and tie.

And if you were a proper lady, you didn't row at all.

Some women rowed locally at the Henley Rowing Club and at a few clubs in London, but their efforts weren't considered all that seriously. As in the U.S., women's efforts to compete in men's sports were at best looked upon with qualified tolerance. In England, attitudes were often more conservative, and Henley was the cradle of rowing tradition. Women were not allowed at the Leander Club, the preeminent rowing and social establishment of the town, founded by Oxford Blues who had graduated and wanted a place to continue their rowing and social affairs. And women were absolutely not allowed to row in the Henley Royal Regatta.

But now in August, things were different at Henley. Aside from the manicured lawns, all of the regalia was gone. The booms and posts were removed and the river and the riverbank were returned to their normal state of placid calm and beauty. The American women had the streets and the river virtually to themselves, for very few Brits got out on the water at the crack of dawn. And despite the closed doors of Leander and the shocked expressions from some of the locals, Henley was still a wonderful place to row.

If a crew team were to close their eyes and visualize a rowing paradise, in fact, the town of Henley and its surroundings might be just what they conjured. Here the Thames River offered lovely stretches of slow-moving water, protected from the wind by tree-lined banks and gently rolling pasture land. Water meadows and weirs helped create an ideal habitat for the several unique species of flowers that lined its banks, as well as the variety of fish that swam in its waters—tench, breem, gundeon, pike, chub, perch, and roach. The beauty of the river called to mind scenes from *The Wind in the Willows*, whose author, Kenneth Grahame, lived downstream, or the poetry of Tennyson, who was married not far upstream at Ship Lake.

Even though Henley was less than thirty miles west of London and shared use of the same river, it stood in marked contrast to the bustling capital. In London, as in most industrial cities, the Thames was still a working river, charted by barges and tugboats, dirtying and roiling its tidal waters within the confines of high sea walls. Oxford and Cambridge rowed their annual duel there, jousting for the best position among the tricky currents, but it was by no means an idyllic spot for rowing.

At Henley, the human element on the river didn't overpower the natural one, but seemed to live in complement to it. Riverside houses often had gardens that reached all the way down to the riverbank, where summer houseboats moored silently along its sides, content to be at rest and restricted to a "walking pace" when they finally decided to move on.

Like the regatta, the pastoral scene on the river was regulated right down to the swans that patrolled its waters. Arching their long necks into a disdainful pose, the swans chased away all other species of waterfowl in their path and didn't budge for even the fastest crew shell. They were royal birds, marked annually with a nick on the beak by Her Majesty's Swan Keepers, men who dressed in red coats every year in a ceremony known as "swan-upping." The swans, however, were about the only nuisance the American oarswomen would have to contend with at Henley.

For one of their first outings, Parker took them on a long scenic row upstream, through the Marsh Locks that marked the confines of Henley. The row was something of an adventure for the crew, something to take their minds off both the rigors of the Boston camp and what still lay ahead. They needed to ship in their oars to fit into the narrow stone locks, and when they got through to the river beyond, it was bounded by beautiful pasture land. When they finally stopped to turn the boat around, there was nothing to break the silence and the lowing of cows, a scene right out of Carie Graves' Wisconsin childhood.

"W-E-L-L," said Chris Ernst suddenly, breaking the Henley spell with her sharp Philadelphia accent, "NOW ISN'T THIS PR-R-R-RETTY!"

SINCE ROWING OUT OF LEANDER was out of the question, the women walked further downstream every morning, along the stretch of race course known as "Henley Reach." There, just past the Remenham Bar, which sat near the two-thirds mark on the course, was another, less conspicuous rowing club. The Upper Thames Boat Club was only a few years old and was completely different from Leander in both character and composition. Upper Thames did allow women members. Its emblem, in fact, was the paired faces of Thamisis and Isis, taken from the reliefs on the Henley Bridge. Leander had a pink hippopotamus.

The Upper Thames boathouse was a low, ranch-like structure with rough-hewn clapboards and a corrugated tin roof. It had a frontier look that made it seem out of place, more appropriate for a river in West Virginia. Or for a group of American pioneers. There, every morning, Harry would join them, having ridden over the river on a borrowed English three-speed bicycle. Harry and his family were staying at one of the private houses that normally volunteered to put up Coach Parker during his visits to Henley.

Henley had always been a good place for Harry Parker. As a competitor, he had first rowed there as a member of the UPenn varsity eight that won the Grand Challenge Cup. Then, in 1959, he had made it to the finals in the Diamond Sculls, and at the same time had met Harvey Love, who'd invited him to come to Harvard. Since then, as a coach, he had taken two or three other crews "across the pond" and done quite well—and this year had been no exception. Although his crew had eventually lost to the British National Team eight in the finals, they had first faced off with Al Rosenberg's U.S. squad and set a new course record.

For Parker, it had been a very satisfying win, a "grudge match" where his coaching superiority had been validated. To Rosenberg and his U.S. eight, however, the face-off had been an unfortunate encounter that may have rattled the confidence of the men's program.

T h i r t e e n

FOR THE U.S. WOMEN, things were only getting better. One of the boons of getting funded for the first time was not only that their plane tickets and lodging had been paid for, but that a brand-new boat had been purchased for them and was waiting in the racks at Upper Thames every morning. Things were looking up. There was even a little money left over in the budget to allow Lynn Silliman's mother, Anne, to come with them, and for Sy Cromwell to come along as the boat rigger.

On the surface, a rigger was supposed to attend to the welfare of the boat itself, to make sure that it was kept in good working order and to repair any problems. He kept the hulls of the wooden boats smooth and well varnished, and quickly repaired any cracks or leaks. A good rigger also kept the undercarriages of the seats clean and oiled, checked the oarlocks for wear, and made sure that none of these moving parts was going to break on race day. Nothing was more devastating than to train as hard and long as a crew did, only to have something break and put the boat out of contention. Beyond a brief allowance after the starter's command, equipment breakage was seen as tough luck. No matter what happened from then on, the race would not be re-rowed.

With a new boat, a rigger usually had to attach and then measure the rigging of the boat to the hull itself, which in a rowing shell referred mainly to the metal armatures that held the oarlock assembly. While certain measurements were held constant in each seat, such as the distance of the oarlocks away from the boat, others, like their height off the water, were customized to each individual. Chris Ernst, for example, sitting in the bow seat, would need to have her oarlock height somewhat lower than Carie or Claudia. Too much height and rowers would be pulling the oars into their necks, too little and they'd be scraping their hands against the gunwales.

The rigger and a coach worked together to this end, and in this area their jobs often overlapped. Harry himself knew a lot about rigging boats; Sy Cromwell knew a considerable amount about both rowing and rowers. Sy was more accessible than Harry in many ways, and most of the women found themselves talking with him about matters outside of the sphere of boat maintenance. If the rigger was the coach's right-hand man, he was often the one the athletes went to for a casual chat. Sy Cromwell wasn't a real rigger, but he had the attributes of one, the rowing background and the penchant to make a big worry small.

One of the first things that Sy Cromwell had to do was to shave down one of the structural ribs or "knees" in the stroke seat. Carie's leg was rubbing up against it so violently that she bled during every practice, baptizing the new boat in blood. Sy and Harry both knew that the fault lay with Carie's rowing more than it did with the boat itself—she had a habit of leaning away from her oar that caused her leg to rub. But both knew that changing the boat was easier than changing Carie, especially at this late point in their training.

The boat that had been ordered for them was a Karlisch, a

beautiful German-made shell with a honey-colored, mahogany hull that was deeper and narrower than the American-built Pococks they'd been rowing back in Boston. While it would take some getting used to, it was unmistakably sleek and fast—a boat that everyone could put their faith in. It was quite a step up from the clunky, decrepit hand-me-downs most of the women had used in their various college programs. Everything fit for once, including the shoes.

A well-made wooden boat was a composition of several different species of wood, each of which had a special quality that contributed to the boat's overall character. They were generally framed in Sitka spruce, skinned with mahogany or cedar, and ribbed with ash. A boat, like the crew itself, was designed to be strong, fast, and lightweight.

George Pocock, the preeminent American boat builder, had been quoted on several occasions as saying that there was no such thing as fast boats, only fast crews. It was true that a good crew would do well in almost any boat, but that was no excuse to put them in anything less than the best. Pocock's shells, elegantly crafted from Western red cedar, had been the most sought after by American crews in their day. Now, more and more on the international level, races were frequently won by less than a second, and the equipment could make a significant difference. New materials like glass fiber were being experimented with, but nothing yet could match the qualities of wood, which was strong and yet resilient.

A local British boat builder had even begun to make boats out of aluminum, and Sy Cromwell tried one out one day. But Cromwell, who had won the Diamonds at Henley in 1964, put a little too much power into the boat and brought the feeble craft back with its riggers bent.

To provide some competition and mark their progress in the new eight, Parker had the crew do pieces with Mike Hart and Chris Baillieu, the British National Team double scull who were also on their way to the Worlds. A men's double was slightly faster than a women's eight and the two boats made for good training partners. The Henley course was well marked every 250 meters, and the crews could get accurate split times, after making allowances for the current.

From their first row in it, Gail Pierson knew that it was a fast boat. She knew that having their own boat, especially one that fit well, was a big psychological boost. Rowers, like bicyclists, were half-human, half-machine, and when the two meshed well, the machine became merely an extension of the athletes, instead of a cumbersome piece of equipment to be suffered.

She also began to realize how smart Harry had been to bring them over here to Henley to train and to have the crew get used to being in a foreign land where things were done a little differently. Even though Henley was much different than Nottingham, it still got them used to the English weather and social climate, and made them feel comfortable enough in it so that they could focus on their own big race. There was more to successful racing than a good boat and well-trained team, and it was here that the Americans and the British differed in their approaches to the sport.

PETER SUTHERLAND, one of the founders of Upper Thames Boat Club, had given Parker and his crew permission to row out of the boathouse, but a young British architect in his firm named Nigel Gallaher had acted as the intermediary. Gallaher had known Harry during his graduate school days at Harvard, enjoying a love–hate relationship with the enigmatic American who coached so differently than the British. Once, after a year's sabbatical at Oxford, Gallaher was out on the Charles in a single scull and crossed paths with Parker near the Anderson Bridge. The two briefly exchanged jibes.

"Now that I'm back at Harvard," Nigel shouted out from his single, "I'll have to relearn the Harvard rowing style!"

Parker paused for a second and then called back over his shoulder, "Nigel, that presupposes you knew what it was to begin with."

For those who knew the history of British and American rowing, the exchange was code language for the long-standing war between the two countries and the way they approached the sport of rowing. It was both a stylistic and an attitudinal difference.

Looking around at Henley one might easily come to the conclusion that the British were the masters of the rowing world, and up until the twentieth century, they had been. Throughout the 1800s, in fact, Great Britain had produced most of the advances in rowing technique and equipment that resulted in the modern sport of rowing. America had contributed some creative ideas, but England had largely perfected them. What began as more or less a recreational activity, done in heavy, wide-beamed, lapstrake hulls, progressed into an Olympic sport carried out in sleek, paper-thin "shells" weighing very little—all in a period of fifty years. Metal outriggers, sliding seats, and swivel oarlocks were the major technical innovations perfected by the British boat builders.

Along with the changes in equipment came the perfection of rowing technique. The metal outriggers, which allowed boats to be made narrower, also necessitated greater balancing skill on the part of the oarsmen. The sliding seat, which allowed the oarsmen's legs to be engaged, required a rethinking of the use of the oarsmen's back and arms. For many years, the English favored a stroke whereby the back was engaged early on to help initiate the stroke; in America the legs were favored more. Numerous books were written on rowing technique, and debates held constantly, but when in doubt everyone generally looked to England. Even George Pocock, the American boat builder who had so greatly influenced the American style of rowing, was himself a Brit, the son of an Eton boat builder.

British rowing, however, had started falling behind, while rowing on the continent and in its former colonies had continued to develop, taking the rowing gospel from the British masters during the early 1900s and infusing it with their own new ideas and energy. Aside from changes in actual technique, perhaps the largest shift made by the new rowing powers was to abandon the amateur ethic, the tacit understanding that rowing—even competitive rowing—was not practiced with the sole intent of winning.

The concept of "professionalism" was still frowned upon by the British rowing establishment. It was crass and it usually signified a lack of class. A person who devoted a disproportionate amount of time and energy to the sport was not considered a proper gentleman. Gentlemen occupied their time with other matters as well as athletics. Sport was essential to the education of an Englishman, but more as a means to a larger end. This was a good perspective, but it had its limitations. And one of the biggest was that it restricted the sport to the upper class.

Women hadn't been the first ones to be discriminated against at Henley.

The amateur rule, begun in 1878, basically forbade those who worked with their hands (mechanics, artisans, laborers) from competitions like Henley. Jack Kelly, one of the finest oarsmen to ever emerge from the U.S., had been forbidden to compete at Henley in 1918 because of it. Kelly, a Philadelphian, owned a bricklaying business, which made him a tradesman in the eyes of the English. When he won the Olympics in Antwerp the next year, he sent his sweaty cap to George III as a gentle rebuff. It wasn't until nearly thirty years later, however, that he got his final revenge, when he returned to Henley to watch his son, Jack Jr., win the Diamond Sculls—the same race from which he had been excluded.

By that time, the old amateur rules had been changed, and the Henley stewards had invited him to come down from the grandstands to help present the award to his son. It was a gesture of goodwill, to help heal an old wound. His daughter was also in attendance that day, the future screen star and Princess of Monaco, Grace Kelly. Prejudice in rowing and the world had indeed begun to lift, when the sons and daughters of a bricklayer could both become noble. But it still had a long way to go.

Jack Kelly, Jr., had gone on to become a supporter of women's rowing. His wife was a former Olympic swimmer and he knew firsthand what a woman could do in athletics. When he had introduced the first black rower into the hallowed halls of Vesper Boat Club, several of the senior members couldn't handle it and quit. A few years later, when he introduced some women into the club, the same thing happened.

The Americans weren't the only ones who began to win medals. Other countries that had learned rowing technique from the British masters had also recently come into their own. After World War II, the Germans in particular turned to the sport with unmatched zeal, as a way to boost national pride and gain Olympic distinction. The Russians and other Eastern Bloc countries also made great strides. They took their rowing lessons from the English, but dismissed the amateur code that came with them. And when the Russian national crews started taking the medals away at Henley, the Brits were not pleased. In a book called *The English Style of Rowing*, authors P. Haig Thomas and M. A. Nicholson lamented the British lack of victories from its opening chapter, "English Rowing in Decline." They blamed it on rival fads in coaching technique and a lack of solidarity among British rowers and their coaches.

Chris Baillieu, the British sculler who was training in the double scull against Harry's women, thought that Henley represented everything that was wrong with British rowing; it had a lot of pageantry but no real substance. Other British rowers pointed to the lack of a "can do" attitude in England that other countries, especially the U.S., seemed to possess. Parker and his American crews were always very "can do." It was a naïve notion, perhaps, to think that a group of relatively inexperienced upstarts could turn themselves into a distinguished crew in such short order, but it was an attitude that fit the country they came from.

Aesthetics off the race course weren't the only thing the British cared about. The term "bad form" applied to rowing as well. When the Brits watched a regatta, they looked not only at who was winning but at the precision of each crew's rowing style. Good rowing should look effortless, like a water ballet, regardless of how hard the crew was actually working. A crew that struggled its way down the course with brute force, swinging wildly at the water as if they held cricket bats not oars, was considered an undignified sight, regardless of whether they won or lost.

Harry Parker was part of a line of unorthodox coaches who questioned the classical English style of rowing—or any "style" that had been set in stone. Parker's own coach, Joe Burk, who had twice won the Diamond Sculls at Henley, was considered an example of this "ungainly" sort of rowing. Instead of incorporating a slow recovery between strokes that imparted a long, graceful glide to the shell, Burk rowed a high, punchy stroke that by no means looked effortless. Burk's rowing had been seen as the precursor to the "Ratzenburg style," the German interpretation of rowing technique that had taken the world by surprise in the late 1950s, and especially at the 1960 Olympics in Rome.

Parker had been in Rome racing in his single, and he had certainly taken note of what the Germans and the Russians were doing.

GAIL PIERSON noticed that one of the things Parker did well was to get his crews ready to race. Part of that preparation obviously had to do with their physical state, with getting them as fit and strong as they could possibly be, without overtraining them. Basically, a coach worked a crew as hard as he could, and then a week or so before their big race, he began to "taper" them, to reduce the intensity and the length of their workouts. Tapering gave everyone's bodies time to fully recuperate, to be well rested for one last maximum effort.

But another equally important part of a crew's final preparation was psychological. This area was often forgotten by other coaches. The key was to set the stage for victory by helping the crew visualize what they were about to do and giving them the right amount and kind of confidence to do it. Indeed if there was one thing that the British and Henley were right about, it was that a rowing race was truly a performance, and needed to be rehearsed with that in mind.

Unlike some coaches, who tried to build confidence by making their crews feel secure and encouraged, Parker always made it a point to keep things organic in his crews, and to allow for changes to occur if the situation called for it. Things changed. People changed. A crew, or a person in a crew, could get stagnant if they were left in the same lineup for too long. There was, of course, a negative consequence to keeping everyone constantly guessing about their seats, scrapping amongst themselves to hold on to their positions. But a crew had to be kept hungry, as well as cohesive. It was a fine balance that had to be maintained. To some, it may have seemed unfair or cruel, but it was definitely a survival of the fittest.

He'd treated these women the same as he treated men. In typical Parker fashion, he had held his cards close to his chest, never telling them how they were doing within the boat or against the ultimate competition. Chris Ernst still felt like she was being seat raced against the starboard spare, Gail Ricketson, and Carie Graves didn't even really know if she was stroking the boat anymore. Harry had pulled her out of the lead seat for a few days and put her in at six. On the starboard side, sometimes Claudia Schneider and Nancy Storrs swapped seats, at three and five. With only a week or so left before the World Championships, such shifting around seemed absolutely crazy. What kind of chess game was Parker playing?

And as far as how well they would do as a team, Parker had kept to his story that they barely belonged in the same water as the top European crews.

But now, as the days passed at Henley, he slowly began to shift this stance. He had always been confident, but now he became filial. He removed the stern, silent mask of the dissatisfied coach, and began to reveal a lighter side of himself. Instead of their taskmaster, he was now more their guardian—rechecking the rigging, making sure they were healthy. He was there to see to their individual needs, to protect and develop their progress as a crew. To some of the women in the boat, starved for goodwill, the emotional turnaround came as a welcome sea-change.

When they had arrived at Henley, many of the crew were worn to the bone. Wiki was sick again, as she had been during camp in Boston, Gail had a sore throat, and even Carie was having a hard time in the stroke seat—and it wasn't simply because of her bloody leg. She felt out of synch with the rest of the crew, as if she had somehow lost her sense of rhythm and couldn't feel the timing of the others behind her. Harry spotted this and pulled her out of the stroke seat, reassuring her that she simply needed a few days respite. When she and Wiki were better, they would return to their seats, refreshed and ready to row well once more.

It was time to taper the team from the hard training now, before they totally burned out. It was also time to keep them from worrying too much about what was coming up at the Worlds. Parker told Chris Ernst not to worry about the size difference between them and the Russians, who were thirty pounds heavier and more than a head taller. "Just don't look at them," he advised. The upstream row through the locks had been one way to divert their attention, as well a side trip to Canterbury Cathedral.

Despite the colds, the team remained in good spirits. The trip had been a wise move, for being abroad, engaged in such singular activity, could only bring them closer together. Henley was working its own magic on them, helping them gel into a real team and get to know each other a little better.

No one really knew Gail Pierson before, because she'd always disappeared after practice on the Charles to her home in Arlington. When Gail came down with a cold at Henley, however, Anne Warner accompanied her to a village pharmacy to get some cough drops. Her Louisiana drawl had proved challenging to the locals, and sometimes she had a difficult time conveying exactly what she wanted. When she asked for some "lozenges," the Englishman behind the counter couldn't understand what she was saying. She repeated the word again and again (*"law zen jes, law zen jes!"*) But the man just shook his head and shrugged, while Anne Warner did her best not to laugh out loud. Gail was the oldest member of the team, the unspoken captain, and sometimes took herself a little too seriously.

She had frowned on her younger teammates' prank of throwing Carol Brown's bra out the hotel window. And one day after practice, she had pooh-poohed a casual boast by Wiki Royden and Chris Ernst that they could probably do about fifteen pull-ups. The two of them had finally confirmed who was stronger by arm-wrestling outside one of the local pubs. Even though it was a good-natured contest that ended in a draw, Gail had looked on with mild disinterest as if she was above such idle play.

Now in Gail's struggle with the pharmacist, Anne Warner decided to do the same.

"Hell!" Gail finally blurted out to the man behind the counter, "Do you have something to suck on?"

WARNER CONCLUDED that Pierson was redeemable after all. She still wasn't sure about Carie Graves, the only one who continued to act somewhat aloof. She retreated to her hotel room whenever they weren't rowing and refused to participate in any of the team's social outings. What was wrong with her? The rivalries between different members of the boat still existed, but they had been tempered by the trip into mild challenges and harmless pranks that were more the earmarks of affection for one another. Carie claimed that the pranks were a private school thing that she couldn't relate to. But she obviously had other things on her mind.

One night, during one of their last days at Henley, Anne Warner thought it might be fun to steal Harry's British bicycle and do something to it. She enlisted Wiki, Chris, Nancy, Carol, and the two Gails. Parker kept his bike in a shed nearby, and an hour before sunrise, they broke in. They were dressed like bandits, with folded handkerchiefs around their faces, and armed with red, white, and blue streamers. They proceeded to decorate Harry's bike garishly, stringing the colored paper through the spokes and attaching long strands to the handle bars.

When the job was finished, they hid nearby and waited for Parker to arrive. While they waited in the darkness, they made secret bets among themselves about how Harry would react. At the Harvard–Yale races every June, Parker's varsity crew would often roast their coach during a mock "play," and he tolerated this as part of tradition. All of this, however, took place within the confines of Red Top, the private grounds in New London, Connecticut, where the Harvard crews trained for their annual race. Here at Henley, they were in the public eye, and his team had already caused a few minor scandals. Now it was Parker's turn to be laughed and gawked at.

When Harry saw the bike, however, he merely grinned, and then acted as if nothing at all was different about it. He wheeled it carefully out of the shed, so as not to disturb the streamers, and proceeded to ride it through the streets of Henley, over the bridge and down to the Upper Thames boathouse. He coached them on it for both practices that day, much to the amusement of both the team and several bystanders, who spotted him while walking along the tow paths. He didn't seem embarrassed by the gaudy, red-white-and-blue bicycle, but instead quite proud.

It was, in a way, a perfect display of his feelings toward this crew—the one that he had been so reluctant to coach only a few months earlier. They might be bold and brash, and something of a joke in the eyes of the traditional rowing community, but Parker had come to enjoy working with them as much as any other crew that he had ever coached. He could never *say* that out loud, but it showed in the way he rode the bike around like a schoolboy on holiday, letting the streamers fly right into his face. Perhaps, in fact, he hadn't let down his guard at Henley as part of any conscious plan. Perhaps the women themselves had opened him up.

In any case, Harry Parker was smiling. And to him, the prank was a clear indication that his team was indeed bonding outside of the boat. More important, a team that could wake up in the middle of the night and wrap streamers around his bike certainly had plenty of energy.

They were ready to race.

F o u r t e e n

WHAT WAS THE BIG SECRET of the Russian and German success? Gail Pierson had once tried to examine their equipment at a regatta in Duisberg by having a teammate take a picture of her standing next to their boat and oars. She concluded that, at least in the case of the Russians, their equipment was actually much worse than their own. The boats were heavy and clunky, but the Russian rowers were so huge and powerful it didn't really matter—they were built more like rugby players than rowers. When the U.S. women arrived at Nottingham, they looked over the course and watched in awe as the Russian women's eight warmed up by pairs, two people pulling the entire boat along at full pressure. It was an exercise that would have broken the backs of the average rower, male or female, and a testimony to the kind of raw power they possessed.

The East Germans were even more impressive. They not only made the best boats in the world, but usually produced the finest oarsmen. Part of this success was due to an early selection process. Athletes for different sports were identified from childhood, based on tests done to determine how tall they would be, how much they would weigh, and even the nature of their muscle fiber—how much fast-twitch versus slow-twitch fiber they possessed. As a result, the East German oarsmen all had more or less the same build, less bulky than the Russians, perhaps, but just as tall and muscular.

The Americans, by contrast, were an odd mishmash—a true representation of the country that had produced them. They ranged in size from the 6-foot 1-inch Carie Graves at stroke, to the tiny 5-foot 4-inch Chris Ernst in the bow seat. They had a seven seat who was old enough to be someone's mother, and a coxswain so young she was *chaperoned* by her mother. Before they got dressed and actually took to the water, some of the other teams even mistook Ernst as a spare coxswain. In their extreme differences in size, personality, and style, they looked more like a track team, or even a troop of circus performers.

And the uniforms they were issued at Nottingham didn't help.

In a sport that had such little equipment to offer, the uniform was a pretty big deal. Individually, it meant you had truly made it, had earned the right to be in the boat. Collectively, the uniforms made you look like a team, not a motley crew or a bunch of hacks. Everyone looked forward to earning their National Team uniform, and it was something to be worn with great pride. The good teams all had impressive uniforms, the mere sight of which could instill fear into their opponents. The East German women always looked distinguished and intimidating in their long black sweat pants and white, long-sleeved jerseys, covered with racing tees that had a tri-color sash of yellow, orange, and black. In the center of the shirt was a war-like black eagle holding its outstretched wings like flexed muscles, the feathers pointy, like the ends of a spear.

The U.S. women's crew, of course, had never *had* real uniforms before, never been funded by their country to compete. It was kind of an exciting moment. The men had great shirts, sleeveless and white, with a handsome U.S.A. patch set into the middle of a horizontal band of red, white, and blue. But because the men's and women's rowing budgets were still separate, the women's wear was designed differently, based on some ideas offered by the Long Beach sculling contingent.

When the crew first saw the uniforms, however, they weren't impressed.

They looked more like gymnastics wear than rowing togs— bright red sleeveless leotards covered by tight-fitting, short shorts. Almost everyone was used to rowing in loose tee-shirts and standard track or gym shorts. The brightly colored, skin-tight uniforms made everyone feel odd and conspicuous; they showed off every muscle and curve and left little to the imagination. Rumor had it that even Tommy Keller, the race director and head of FISA (the Fédération Internationale des Sociétès d'Aviron, the international governing body of rowing) had referred to the U.S. women's outfits as "clown suits" when he saw them for the first time.

The team had already been feeling insecure about their physical presence, and now they had to wear these odd costumes. They seemed unfinished somehow, or thrown together at the last minute. The shirts had no stars or stripes, just a simple U.S.A. stitched across the front, to break up the field of bright red. Even the socks issued to them were objectionable, tennis peds that had little balls sewn onto the top of the heels. Didn't they know that rowers always wore wool socks to keep their feet dry? Whoever designed these things, Carie thought, ought to be shot.

The California scullers who had helped design the uniforms, however, hadn't intended to make a bad fashion statement—just develop an outfit that wouldn't interfere with their rowing. Baggy shorts could get caught in the seat tracks, loose shirts could trap the oar handles or even the thumbs. Their intentions were good— in fact ahead of their time. Twenty years later crew "unitards" that looked a lot like these strange, new uniforms would be standard issue.

Claudia Schneider, whose Long Beach crew had adopted leotards that year, had grown used to them and knew they were comfortable to row in, especially in the heat of late August. In terms of fashion, she actually thought they made the U.S. team look more like *women*, not amorphous bodies in men's clothes. The East and West Germans were covered from head to toe: what did they have to hide?

Chris Baillieu and Mike Hart, the British double, had one explanation to offer—they were certain that some Eastern Bloc teams were using steroids, or male hormone injections. During World War II, the Germans had first started experimenting with steroid use, as a way to make soldiers stronger, more aggressive, and more oblivious to pain. Steroid use in sports had been banned, and at Nottingham for the first time ever, drug tests would be administered to both male and female athletes. But there were ways to trick the tests, by abstaining from steroids at just the right time so that you could escape detection.

The Americans certainly *looked* different than the East Germans and the Russians, who were strong but also bulky. The Germans outweighed the Americans by an average of twenty pounds a person, the Russians even more. But despite the weight difference and all their various heights, the Americans looked "ripped," a weightlifting term for a body that showed every muscle fiber when flexed. If the Americans were practically the only team out there that looked like women, there was also no mistaking the fact that they were serious athletes. By now their bodies had the lean and well-defined muscles that came to a rower at the end of a hard season.

And when they got on the water and actually began to row, their muscles jumped to attention and provided any spectator with a lesson in human anatomy. Their forearms and triceps were the envy of any sailor; their deltoids flexed like striated shoulder pads; their lats, the triangular muscle that connected the arms to the back, fanned out over the shoulder blades and made you believe that humans could indeed sprout wings. Who needed fancy uniforms, when the body itself could provide such impressive detail?

CARIE, AT LEAST, HAD OTHER THINGS TO DO than to worry about the team uniforms. Arthur Grace had arrived, having persuaded some poor editor at *Time* magazine that the U.S. women's crew, a completely unknown quantity and of questionable news value, merited sending him to England to shoot. His sudden appearance and then absence from her life had been emotionally trying, and it had made the trip to Henley less enjoyable than it should have been. Instead of bonding with the rest of the team as some of the others did, she had spent much of the time off the water in her hotel room, writing letters, reading, and missing Arthur.

Carie didn't consider herself to be someone who spent much time worrying about boyfriends. Ironically, she remembered how she'd been to Nottingham before, two years ago, at the start of her European sojourn. Then, too, she'd been with a boyfriend, but she'd soon left him and struck out on her own. Men were expendable when they conflicted with her larger plans. She was a different person then, a wanderer and a loner, willful but unfocused. Now, in a very short space of time, she'd become very determined to achieve something important and precise through her rowing. How did Arthur fit into the picture? She hadn't planned on meeting someone like him, someone whose effect on her was so powerful that it threatened to send her off the course she'd set for herself.

She wasn't sure what she was going to do with Arthur, but she was certainly happy that he had arrived.

ARTHUR GRACE wasn't the only one waiting for the team in Nottingham, the home of Sherwood Forest and Robin Hood. The U.S. women's team manager, Tina Bayer, and her mother, Ernestine, had flown in from Philadelphia with the Vesper four. Tom McKibbon's double and quad scullers had also come in from Long Beach—some of the same women that Gail Pierson had once rowed with before she'd defected to sweep rowing and Parker's eight.

If Gail was a revolutionary in women's rowing, then Ernestine Bayer was one of its pioneers. Ernestine had started the Philadelphia Girls Rowing Club at a time when women weren't supposed to row at all, well before Title IX could legally justify a woman's presence on the water. Taught how to scull by her husband, Ernie, she had received a somewhat less cordial welcome from many of the male rowers on the Schuylkill than Gail Pierson had been given on the Charles. Some of the rowing blue bloods had actually told her to stay off the river in threatening tones. Needless to say, she hadn't, and her confrontations both on and off the water had made her known as a force to be reckoned with. Ernestine's crews had made some of the first attempts to compete overseas, and she had strong ideas about women's rowing. Although her daughter was the official team manager, she took her role as a doyenne quite seriously.

She did not like some of the things she saw happening with Parker's crew, like the evening revelry of certain rowers. Some, like Claudia Schneider and Carie Graves, were even sneaking out of the college dorms to have a beer or cavort with the Australian men's team. In an effort to put a halt to this, she tried to institute certain "training rules" among them, and even set up her room nearby and left her door open to ensure that these were followed. Rowers were required to sign out of their dorms and report exactly where they were going.

Reunited with Arthur, Carie as well as her cohorts had no intention of being told what to do. Ernestine Bayer might indeed be a revered figure in the world of women's crew, but they, too, had paid their dues, had achieved the rank of international class athletes by virtue of hard work, sacrifice, and self-discipline. Harry

Parker had never needed to stand over them with a whip, dictating rules of behavior and conduct. No one else needed to either. If Carie disliked private school pranks, she detested even more the disciplinary measures that often accompanied them.

Carie brought the matter directly to Harry, and Parker instructed the Bayers to back off. His women had enough to worry about, trying to maintain their composure faced with the Russians and the East Germans, without having someone from their own program getting on their nerves.

F i f t e e n

IN TERMS of what they had to do physically, nothing would change; on a psychological level, however, the World Championships would be radically different than anything they had ever done before. Harry had prepared them as best as he could, but the pressure of racing at an international versus a collegiate level was like the difference between performing a high school play and that same play on a Broadway stage. Hearts would race wildly and the distractions would be multiplied. To his young American crew, there were so many unknowns. Most of their racing had been limited to dual competitions, not the six-boat format. And a six-boat race required completely different psychology.

A dual race had a purity to it, just as did boxing, a tennis match, or any competition where two opponents went head-to-head. Dual races, like Henley and the Harvard–Yale race, were the oldest kind of boat race, and they had a very straightforward psychology to them: *beat or be beaten.*

True, this mano-a-mano format often led to some very poor performances. If another crew "broke" their opponent—established enough dominance early in the race—it often took away the other team's will to pull hard, and the margins between the two crews could be big. But a dual race could also provide some very close, exciting performances, when crews mentally "locked horns" with one another, using each other's energy to maintain a deadlock.

Six-boat races had a few other things going for them. First, from the spectators' point of view, they were a visual feast, a brilliant flurry of activity. It was this sort of race that Carie had attended as a child, when she watched her father row at the 1956 National Championships. From a practical standpoint, six-boat races were also a quick way to weed out the slower crews. If the ten women's eights entered at Nottingham had to race each other, two at a time, at least eight separate races would be required to establish the eventual winner. Even then, all of the boats wouldn't get a chance to race each other.

With the multiple-boat format, two heats of five crews would race on Friday. The winner of each heat would proceed directly to the Sunday final. Everyone else would race again in the Saturday repechages—a French word that literally meant "repetition." The repechages would be two races made up of four boats each. These reps would also remix the field, grouping the second- and fourth-place finishers from one heat with the third and fifth from the other, giving everyone an opportunity to race more crews. The top two crews from each repechage would join the final field on Sunday, thus filling all six lanes.

The first heat would pit the mighty East Germans against Romania, West Germany, Holland, and Great Britain. The Americans had been placed in the second heat, along with Russia, Hungary, Poland, and France. The Russian crew, of course, was the favorite, but the American women knew they couldn't get caught up worrying about any one crew, because another boat might come along and completely surprise them.

Carie had experienced this scenario firsthand at the Women's Nationals from the other vantage point, when her young Wisconsin varsity eight had surprised the veteran crews off the starting line and then desperately held on to the lead. The bold move had forced the better crews to play a game of catch-up with a boat they had not considered a strong opponent. And seeing an upstart crew row beside or just ahead of you could send even a good crew into a tailspin of doubt, forcing them to question their assumptions and their worth.

If a six-boat race had a different psychology to it, it did offer opportunities for an underdog. Wisco had proven this in Princeton. Perhaps the U.S. team could pull off an upset here, too. The odds were certainly stacked against them in terms of size, experience, and race preparation. But the U.S. *was* wearing bright red, just like the Wisconsin team had worn.

YOU MIGHT THINK that after training muscles for so long, repeating the same motion again and again, a crew race would be relatively easy—that the muscles would have their own memory and could simply take over while the mind sat back and went on automatic pilot. After all, who needed to worry with a coxswain like Lynn Silliman to steer and do all the strategic thinking? Unlike other sports, where the mind had to be prepared for any number of different scenarios, rowing was relatively pure and simple: *Just pull hard.*

This essential purity had attracted Carie to the sport; rowing was about as stripped down as an athlete could get in terms of physical effort. And yet, as she found out early on, this quality also made it more intense, made the connection to the mind closer, not farther away. Besides, in a boat your mind had plenty to worry about, even though these concerns were unapparent to the spectators, or even sometimes the rowers themselves. These were the subtle, tactile skills of keeping your feel for the water, of keeping in rhythm with the rest of the crew, of keeping your mind in the boat when it really didn't want to be there at all, because being there meant feeling the pain of the muscles, crying for oxygen, being pushed to maximum on every stroke.

As she thought about the race, she worried. The race would be painful—that was a given. But the real question for her was, could she get back her sense of rhythm?

IT WOULD TAKE A FEW YEARS for Anne Warner to figure out why Harry Parker had chosen Carie Graves, instead of her or Wiki Royden, to sit in the stroke's seat. The revelation finally came to her off the water, away from the world of crew, when Anne was directing a Slavic women's choir back in Cambridge. She had invited Carie to be a member of the a cappella choir, and had been pleasantly surprised to discover that, despite a lack of formal musical training, her old rowing rival had a rich alto voice.

Even with this discovery, however, Anne couldn't quite figure out how to use Carie in the choir. Carie was fine singing alone, but she lacked the skills to harmonize or hold her own part among the others. Still, she did have that remarkable alto voice, so finally Anne decided that the only place to put her was out in front, as a soloist. Standing alone, detached from the rest of the choir, Carie would usually begin the song in a key of her own choosing (a starting note would be provided, but often ignored). Then, after her solo was nearly over, the rest of the group would join in behind her, silently hoping that Carie had left them on a note close enough to their vocal range.

This was a bizarre way to orchestrate things, but it worked amazingly well. Anne found that it was better to let Carie go untethered, not to inhibit her raw talent, even though it sometimes challenged those who had to follow behind her.

This, she surmised, was exactly the conclusion Parker had come to: *Let a wild horse run free.*

CARIE STROKED a crew the way she sang in a choir: strong and certain, but often beginning on the wrong note. And just as she had in the heats at Princeton, she went off the line for their heat on Friday too excited, too fast. That would have been all right, they'd still have had a chance to settle down, except that Lynn's electronic speaker system suddenly quit and no one could hear a word she was saying. Without Lynn's voice, they were completely in the dark— they didn't know where they were and what they needed to do.

Fortunately, this soon became a moot point. For despite the fury of Carie's rushed stroke rating, the Americans easily shook off the crews on either side of them. There was only one crew still with them. Far off to their left, also dressed in red, were the Russians. To be matching strokes with the U.S.S.R.—it was almost inconceivable. Now they didn't need a coxswain to tell them where they were or what they needed to do. At 500 meters, they were less than a second behind them, a distance of only a quarter boat-length.

Before the race, Anne Warner, a Russian studies major, had overheard the Russian coach berating his team with the words: "You must win!" He kept repeating this over and over again like a chant, until he noticed Anne watching him with a bemused expression. She had tried to talk to the Russian oarswomen earlier, but they had clearly been instructed not to speak to anyone. The Russian coach quickly lowered his voice, and conducted the rest of his sermon in private.

Looking at the Russians now, going into the last forty strokes of the race, you didn't have to speak their language to see that the giant rowers were dying, gasping for breath with every stroke. The U.S. boat was working hard, too, but certainly not at maximum. Part of this was because they still didn't know their full potential and didn't have preconceived notions of where they should be in relation to the other boats. It was, after all, only their first race together in that lineup. The other reason was that Carie had taken the rating up too high, so that everyone in the boat was rushing the slides—coming up to each catch a little too fast. Although it seemed counterintuitive, a faster rating could actually cause a crew to go slower, to spin its wheels and not be able to get good purchase on each stroke.

When the crews crossed the line, the American women finished behind the Russian crew by four-tenths of a second, a blink of an eye. Anne Warner looked over at the boat that had just beaten them. Instead of jubilant, ecstatic faces, she saw shocked expressions, filled with pain. Suddenly a few of the Russian women leaned over and threw up over the side of the boat.

Despite having won, the Russians were in a state of utter exhaustion. They had never counted on having to row so hard during the first heat, hadn't expected the Americans to be so competitive. The U.S. crews had always been pushovers before, had never even made the six-boat final. Suddenly the Russians didn't seem so big to Anne anymore. If they were that tired after barely beating them, something was wrong. Either that, or the U.S. was much faster than they had imagined.

In her own boat, there were nine shocked women, too, but their astonishment was edged with quiet excitement. They had rowed a mediocre race with an out-of-control stroke and a broken speaker system—and almost won. Suddenly everyone in the boat began to wonder the same thing: could they actually make it to Sunday's final? In the other heat, predictably, the East Germans had won, beating Romania, West Germany, Holland, and Great Britain. That meant the Russians and the East Germans would get the next day off, to rest up for the final. The Americans along with everyone else would proceed to the repechages and a second chance to qualify.

A DAY'S REST might be a good thing for an experienced boat, but for a young group like the U.S., another race meant another chance to learn something. After all, they had not actually raced well in the first heat, despite their near victory. If they could figure out how to relax and row with more composure, who knew *what* might be possible. This, in essence, is what Harry Parker told them—no longer that they didn't belong with the Russians and the Germans, but that they were capable of being the fastest crew out there.

The next day, with a renewed sense of confidence and calm, they rowed the repechage exactly to plan—staying long and relaxed, with more time between strokes. Carie had never rowed a race like this, controlling the entire field behind her with such ease. They led the rest of the field by four seconds, nearly a full boat-length over West Germany and Poland. They had open water over Great Britain, another women's program just struggling to get started. In the other heat, Romania and Holland battled it out, pulling away from Hungary and France. Even though all the repechage times were slower than Friday's heats, the U.S. had posted the fastest one of the day, a 3:21.11, compared to Romania's 3:22.22. Things were definitely looking up.

But now another opponent had arrived uninvited—the wind.

S i x t e e n

〜〜〜〜〜〜〜〜〜〜〜〜

THE ROWING COURSE at the Holme Pierpont National Water Sports Center resembled a giant outdoor swimming pool. Dug out of a former gravel pit, a million cubic meters of muck had been removed to create the rectangular body of water touted in the race program as an ideal site for elite rowing competition. Its dimensions were set to FISA/international standards for fair racing, with lanes set 13.5 meters apart and 3.5 meters deep. The banks even had a textured surface in order to dissipate waves, not bouncing them back into the middle of the race course which would make things difficult for the rowers. The banks were also set at a wide angle in relation to the bottom of the artificial lake, to minimize the effects of wave motion and drag.

To ensure fairness at the starting line, special platforms or stake boats had been made for both the 2000-meter start of the men's races and the 1000-meter start for the women, adjustable to boats of any length. At the finish line there was a three-story control tower, where the judges could sit and let the electronic timer sort out the times and places, flash them up on an electronic scoreboard, and consult state-of-the art photo finish equipment if need be. The tower was connected to a main reception building for the athletes, where the judges could stroll over and have afternoon tea between races.

By reading the race program, a spectator could see that considerable thought had been put into the design of the course, based on research done at Southampton University and by studying the features of the 1972 Olympic course in Munich.

What the program failed to mention was that the rowing site was created and funded by the local Nottinghamshire county council as part of a larger plan—to produce a multifunctional water-sports center. Rowing was just one part of the project. Hidden by the low banks surrounding the race course lay areas for water-skiing, white-water kayaking, fishing, and sailing. The general plan was to satisfy a large group of recreational water-sport users, and separate the activities as much as possible. The inherent problem with this plan, of course, was that the ideal conditions for rowers were radically different than those of sailors.

Sailors reveled in wind, while rowers despised it.

Rumor had it that prior to the center's creation in 1973, the same area had been considered as a possible site for the East Midlands airfield. This plan had been abandoned because the winds in the area were determined to be too strong and unpredictable. To combat the negative effects of wind, the rowing-course designers had built up the banks around the race course. The size and shape of the banks had been "scientifically determined" to eliminate any adverse turbulence. The course had been dug in an east–west orientation, in the direction of the prevailing winds. That way, in theory, the headwind confronting the rowers would be equal and fair for all.

The reality unfortunately proved otherwise.

Al Rosenberg, whose U.S. men's heavyweight eight was slated to race one week after the women's races, described the effect of the wind on the course as being like a violent storm in an artificial ocean. And when the wind blew the wrong way, across the course, it made the lanes completely unfair. While the banks did indeed shield lanes 1 and 2, the rest of the field was largely unprotected.

In short, when the wind blew hard, the rowers were exposed to some of the worst rowing conditions of any major regatta.

Still, despite some problems at the British national championships, the course's designers hoped for a favorable debut in the 1975 Worlds. Banners of corporate sponsors were strung along the far bank of the course near the finish line, with the giant electronic scoreboard behind them. Sponsors had been successfully courted, a difficult task in a sport that had such a limited base of spectators. Rowing events were seldom televised. A few larger companies like Xerox had been brought on board as well as several local advertisers, like the Guardian Royal Exchange. Another banner hung from the top of the Holme Pierpont Center, as well as several identical ones along the boathouse and waterman's center, which read, "Sport for all."

It should have read, "Wind for all."

THE WIND was waiting for the American women when they arrived at the Holme Pierpont course on Sunday, along with their five adversaries: Romania, W. Germany, Holland, Russia, and East Germany. Wind added an element of chaos to rowing that favored the more experienced crews. Rowing in heavy wind was like walking a tightrope while someone continuously shook the rope or kept hitting your balancing pole. The wind, and the waves that it created, buffeted a crew shell and threatened to throw it off keel. When the balance went off, the blades could hit the water between strokes and wreak further havoc with the balance or "set." And when the set went off, the rowing itself got sloppy, slowing the hull speed of the boat down even more.

The women's eight final was slated to start at five o'clock, the last event of the day. As the biggest and fastest boats on the water, eights were always left for the finale. At this point the few American spectators in the stands hadn't had much to see. All the other U.S. women's crews that rowed earlier had failed to get any medals. The Vesper four had finished last, the quad from Long Beach fifth. The double and the pair hadn't even made the final, and rowed in a second-tier race called the "petites." Even Joan Lind, the talented U.S. sculler, had only managed fifth. So far, the American boats were turning in typical, sub-par performances. The eight was not only the last boat, but the last hope.

The rowers quietly took their wooden boat off its rack, shouldered it, and walked it down to the dock. When they rolled it over and down to the water, a pleasant surprise lay within it. One of the managers from the Long Beach squad named Debbie D'Angelis had tied a single red rose into the laces of each of their shoes. It was a small, wonderful gesture that almost made up for the silly leotards, and a perfect way to launch their last race together. The red roses were the same color as their uniforms, and they decided to keep them in the boat for the race. No matter what happened, they had already gained recognition and a sense of achievement for going further than any American women's eight had gone before. The result of the final was up to fate.

The crews were sent out briefly and then called back in. The wind was simply too strong. It was rare to postpone a regatta. A crew race would be held in rain or snow, but if the race was held in high winds, there was the possibility of swamping. When a boat swamped, things could get messy. The crew generally wasn't at risk unless the water was cold or someone couldn't swim. The wooden boat and oars floated, and if the rowers stayed with the boat, there was generally no real danger.

Chris Ernst and Anne Warner knew about a boy who had died at Yale when his crew had hit an old water-ski ramp. It was October, and he'd tried to swim ashore, but in the cold water he'd cramped up and never made it. While at Radcliffe, Wiki Royden had swamped once at Canadian Henley, just before her crew made it to the finish line. As the strongest swimmer in the boat, she'd promised to save the coxswain, whose own ability to float was in question. Once a boat filled with water, it would hover just below the surface, turning into a floating bathtub. A swamped crew was more of a nuisance for the race officials, who would have to rescue the rowers without damaging their boats. And six swamped boats would cause a huge delay.

While they were waiting for the wind to die down, the Americans placed their boat on the grass beside the race course, upside-down in low slings. Wiki and Anne lay under the overturned boat, gazing at the roses tied into the shoes, and using it as a makeshift cabana against the sun. To combat further illness, they were all popping vitamin C tablets like candy, and swallowing glycerin drops to keep their mouths from going dry. These may not have been as good as steroids, but they were a useful placebo nonetheless.

The time spent waiting passed slowly. Despite what the mind tried to convince the heart and body to do, a racing situation triggered the body's primitive reflexes—the flow of adrenaline and the fight-or-flight survival mechanism. Ironically, Gail Pierson, who had more racing experience than anyone, seemed to actually be suffering the worst. Her heart rate had started to skyrocket, causing her breathing to get short, and her mind was in a state of near panic. She went off alone to try to calm down with some breathing exercises that she'd found useful in the past. Harry Parker, too, had disappeared, leaving the team to deal with their own demons.

Wiki looked at the roses to pass the time and chatted casually with Anne Warner. The two college rivals had become close over the summer, especially as roommates during their stay at Henley. And Carie Graves had found an odd diversion for herself—she went around pulling the balls off of everyone's team-issued tennis peds. When the call finally came for them to race and the boat was again made ready, Carie strode up to Chris Ernst in the bow seat and threw the pompoms into her lap.

"Here, have some extra balls!" she said. "Become a member of the extra balls rowing club!"

To Chris, who was always a bundle of nerves up in the bow, it was just about the best thing anyone could say.

I T   W A S   S I X   O ' C L O C K before the U.S. team finally shoved off, the last crew to depart from the dock. The wind had subsided and was now westerly at two knots, providing a light tail wind that would actually make the rowing easier. The late summer sun had already begun to set over the finish line, and it cast a golden, hazy glow over the man-made hummocks along the banks and on the backs of the rowers as they came down the course.

It wasn't until they were well out onto the practice lane, doing their warm-up starts, that Gail Pierson realized something was wrong. Where were the other boats? Quickly she glanced over her shoulder and saw them lining up for the final, backing into the anchored stake boats.

The stake boats that the British had built weren't boats at all, but an ingenious row of six moveable finger piers, all of which connected to a main dock that nearly ran across the entire width of the course. At the end of each finger dock was a plank, extending out like a low diving board. A boy dressed in jeans and a white shirt lay down on each plank and reached out to grasp the stern of each crew, to hold it there until the starting commands were given. Because the boats weren't exactly the same length, the starter then instructed a second boy to extend or pull in the moveable finger dock, thus lining up the bows of the crews perfectly.

While this alignment was happening, the coxswain of each crew was busy keeping their boat on point, centered in their own lane. In windy conditions, this task was particularly challenging, and if an eight went off the line crooked, the coxswain would immediately lose time and speed correcting the boat's course. Thus, just before the race began, the coxswains who were still adjusting their course held their hands aloft, indicating to the starter they weren't quite ready. When all the hands were down, the race would begin.

When Gail glanced back and saw the hands of the coxswains held aloft, readying themselves like bronco riders, she knew that they were in trouble.

"WAY ENOUGH AND TURN US AROUND!" she yelled at Lynn. "WE'RE GOING TO MISS THE RACE!"

The Americans had been so distracted by the delay of the race that they hadn't heard the call to the line. Quickly, they spun the boat around, the port side backstroking and the starboards rowing. A sixty-foot-long shell, however, isn't designed to turn in place, and the maneuver seemed to take forever. As they sped off toward the starting line, Gail could only hope the other crews were having trouble settling into the stake boats. God, this was the last thing the crew needed before the final. If they hadn't been on pins and needles already, rushing down to the start made certain they would be.

But surely they wouldn't start the race without them, would they?

Nearing the line, she saw that this was exactly what was going to happen. The five other boats were all lined up; the starter was calling out to each of them. No one seemed to care that the Americans weren't there in the empty lane. In good FISA fashion, they were going to start on time—with or without them.

To come this far and not to race. It was impossible, Gail thought. The crew would forever be a laughing stock, the ones who had literally missed the boat. Something had to be done. But what? Even rowing at full tilt, they were still a good thirty or forty strokes from the line; and in the time it would take them to circle around and come up into place, the three-minute race would practically be over. Then she came up with a radical idea.

"CUT ACROSS THE COURSE!" she instructed Lynn.

Using the small rudder that controlled the boat's steering,

Lynn swung them diagonally across the race course, directly in front of the other boats. Turned sideways, the long boat suddenly presented a formidable obstacle for at least two of the lanes—and forced the starter to abandon his effort to begin the race without them. A brief moment of confusion followed, and then the starter yelled at them to quickly pull into position.

For interrupting the race, they were assessed one false start. Two false starts and a crew would be disqualified. That meant they would have to go off the line conservatively, but that was all right. At least they would race.

The U.S. strategy was basic: come off the line at forty strokes a minute, settle twice (to make sure that Carie actually *did* settle), and row the body of the race at a 36. They'd stay long and powerful and not get rushed. Then for the last twenty strokes, they'd crank up the stroke rating again, when Lynn gave the command, "Do it now!" That's when they'd take a crack at the Russians. Perhaps they'd surprise them this time.

The boats were lined up, the rowers poised and silent. Their torsos leaned forward over their bent legs, arms outstretched, like sprinters waiting for a gun to go off. And if only there *was* a gun, instead of the formal French commands that seemed to take forever to be spoken. Then their still legs would become pistons, burning from the exertion of driving down 100 times without relent. But at least after that it would all be over. The waiting was far worse than the race itself.

"ÊTES-VOUS PRÊTES . . ." the starter's voice began. But before he finished, the Russian crew jumped off the start, taking a few other crews along with them. Now the boats had to all be lined up again. It was another delay, and it made things even more nerve-wracking. But at least now the Americans weren't the only ones who had to be careful going off the line.

When the crews were realigned, the starter tried again. "ÊTES-VOUS PRÊTES? . . . PARTEZ!" It was a clean start.

On either side of the course, the coaches watched as the

orderly array of six crews suddenly broke into a jumble of forty-eight swinging bodies and oars, churning up the water behind them. The boats themselves slid back and forward against each other, trading the lead on every stroke. It was like watching the start of a marathon, just a mass of bodies jostling to break free.

Inside each crew, there was a controlled frenzy, an effort to block out the surrounding chaos and keep the focus within the boat. The Americans especially, who had so little experience together as a crew, could not forget this was their main task. A 1000-meter race, with an average stroke rating between 36 and 40, amounted to a mere 120 strokes to sum up all of one's skill and effort, the hundreds of miles of training, the relentless battling among the members of the crew. With so few strokes in which to prove oneself, each one had to count—each had to have both intensity and precision. Unlike in many other sports, where there was always an opportunity to get back in the game, rowing had a real finality to it. A few bad strokes could easily cost you the whole race.

Something had clearly happened to the Russians, for after the first forty strokes they weren't even in the picture. Perhaps their false start had made them begin too cautiously. Perhaps they were trying a new strategy. In any case, they sat about a boat length behind the Americans, who had come off the line without restraint. And a boat length was a hard distance to make up, even for a strong crew.

By 500 meters, or the halfway mark, the six-boat field had separated into two distinct races. The Russians, the West Germans, and the Dutch, in lanes 1, 2, and 3, had all slid back to nearly a boat length behind the leaders: East Germany, the United States, and Romania. Romania was clearly in third place, but unless you were actually rowing in the boat, it was hard to tell who the leader was, East Germany or the United States.

Wiki Royden had always felt that she could look out of the boat and still stay in time with the rest of her teammates. As a sculler, she had needed to look out and see where she was going, and the habit had become ingrained. Anne Warner, rowing behind her in the four seat, would sometimes yell at her when she looked out of the boat. But it really didn't matter, she thought; besides, Gail Pierson sometimes looked out too. One of the drills that Harry made them do was to actually close their eyes and *feel* the rest of the boat, not to rely on the eyes to keep in time. If she could row blind, she thought, then she could certainly use her eyes to peek over at the East Germans.

When she glanced over to her right, only twenty feet away, she found herself looking directly across at the seven seat of the East German boat. *One seat down*, she thought. That was less than one second. Lynn had told them as much, but to see it for herself—the boat they had to beat—helped her turn the race into a personal, one-on-one battle that a single sculler loved. That's what motivated her the most.

The danger of focusing on the East Germans, of course, was that the Romanians, just off to their left, were still within striking distance going into the final sprint. They seldom missed getting a medal at the Worlds. But now, psychologically at least, the race had turned into a two-boat battle, the U.S. against the East Germans. No one else mattered, and both crews knew it. Mentally they had locked horns and were drawing energy from each other—pushing themselves to the breaking point and beyond the reach of the other crews.

Carie Graves never looked out of the boat, especially not during such a close battle. When things got tough, she put her head down and went deep down into the basement of her mind. It was a place where she could draw enormous power, but it sometimes frightened her because of the visions that surfaced. Arthur Grace had captured Carie's striking, intense look many times—the clenched teeth, the piercing dark eyes—but even he hadn't guessed the nightmarish reality that she could enter. Sometimes she hallucinated that she was a soldier, stalking the Khmer Rouge through a marshy grassland, a gun slung over her shoulder. Her thoughts became trained on her own survival, and anger, not fear, was the emotion that ruled her.

She wanted not to run from this enemy, but to kill it. And she barely heard Lynn Silliman's command.

"DO IT NOW!" she shouted. The final sprint.

The wooden boat surged, trying to follow Carie's lead and shift into a higher gear. But they were already at the limits of their power. Their lungs felt like they were on fire, their quadriceps felt the ice-pick-like pain, and a sickening nausea had entered their stomachs. This should have been the breaking point for one of the crews, but both refused to give up the fight—the connection to one another. From the grandstand the boats seemed to cross the finish line together—one crew overlaid almost perfectly against the other. Even spectators standing right at the finish line, looking across the course, could barely distinguish the members of one crew from the other.

Then, like two boxers going into a clinch, the rowers suddenly ceased all motion and let their bodies slump over idle oars. Their boats continued to drift aimlessly forward until they came to a slow halt. All poise abandoned, some of the women fell back into each other's laps, while others let go of their oars and grasped the gunnels, mouths open wide, trying to find a comfortable way to rest while their chests heaved and their hearts continued to race, their bodies screaming for lost oxygen.

Neither crew had delivered the knockout punch, but this time the East Germans would get the clock's judgment—1.6 seconds ahead of the Americans.

CREW RACES end too soon, like a dream interrupted. But for the rowers who row the race, it is a moment of pure salvation. Some collapse, others shout for joy, and some close their eyes in silent prayer. In the slow seconds that passed while they waited to paddle into the awards dock and receive their medals, Wiki Royden gazed out of the boat at the diminishing waves. Her breathing and the wild beating of her heart had finally almost returned to normal. Now she was completely free to look out, to let her mind wander, without the reprimand of the coxswain or the coach, without the critique from one of her teammates.

After the frenzy of the race, it felt good to just sit there and do nothing but stare out at the waves. Each individual wave, she thought, looked like any other, and the waves were like the days that had gone by this summer—days of rowing and training hard that were now all mixed up in her mind and indistinguishable from one another. This day, she concluded, that had passed by so quickly was like one of the many waves that now danced around the boat. It was just a day, like any other. But at some point in the future, she sensed it would rise up and stand much higher than all the rest—like a mountain in her life.

At present, however, there were still so many questions that kept running through her mind. They had come so far so soon, and now it was suddenly all over. The electronic scoreboard displayed the race results with a cold and formal finality. Would they row into the dock and put the boat away and never see each other again? Or would this just be the beginning of things, a preview of the first Olympics next year. And what would Harry think, back at the dock? Was second place good enough for him?

All of these doubts were put aside for the moment as the team rowed up to the awards platform. There Tommy Keller, the head of FISA, was standing on the dock looking absolutely radiant, dressed in a navy blazer and white cotton trousers. The Americans weren't clowns anymore in his or anyone's eyes, but one of the best crews in the world—perhaps *the* best, if you believed that the East Germans had used steroids. Cameras flashed as Keller carefully hung the silver medals around their necks. As each one of their heads bowed in turn, they looked like they were being knighted. Then, he formally shook their hands. Apparently Keller had become fast friends with Nancy Storrs' father, who had taken the red-eye to London and then driven straight on to Nottingham to see his daughter row. With no sleep and a few beers in him, Storrs now felt giddy enough to rush onto the dock, steal a kiss from Lynn Silliman, and then pretend to nearly push Keller into the water. At this, the women broke up into laughter.

They shoved away, put on their white warm-up shirts, and then joined the other five finalists for a victory paddle over the last part of the course. The boats were supposed to finish in order of the way they had just placed, so that more photos could be taken for the local papers. Only the Germans noticed, too late, that somehow the American boat had edged by them, crossing over the finish line first. Had Carie Graves been able to speak German, she might have told them that she never paddled easy, it made her butt hurt.

Back at the dock, a small band of supporters waited for them. Sy Cromwell, Bernie Horton, Lynn's mother Ann, and of course, Harry Parker. Their quiet, reserved coach didn't quite know what to do. Usually, his victorious Harvard crews grinned and shook hands with one another, or slapped each other on the back—an occasional whoop or holler might be heard. But as soon as his women got out of the boat, they immediately ran around screaming and hugging each other, eyes welling up with tears. Even Gail Pierson, the elder statesmen of the group, suddenly sprang into a handstand on the dock.

As Parker stiffly embraced each one of them in turn, a very un-Parker-like expression slowly began to spread across his face. It began with a huge grin, which grew bigger and bigger until it broke into an unbridled, toothy smile. It was a look of almost pure joy, and it mirrored what he saw in his team's eyes.

Epilogue

IN ROWING, explaining the success of an underrated crew is almost as difficult as accounting for the poor performance of a highly favored one. Harry Parker had always been fascinated by the more mysterious elements that made some boats go fast—and others slow—despite the size and experience of the people in them. It was one of the things, in fact, that kept him coaching crew for so long. Sometimes, the parts didn't add up to the whole, despite all the careful calculations.

This women's team, the one he had just watched match the East Germans right down to the wire, was a case where the whole was much greater than the sum of its parts. For anyone in the know, sitting in the stands, this had made the race even more thrilling to watch. No one matched strokes like that with the East Germans, especially not a crew that had come out of nowhere. And what had happened to the Russians?

Second best in the world. The women themselves were just beginning to figure out what they'd done. Claudia Schneider, who spoke fluent German, befriended some of the East German rowers and secretly swapped gear with them behind the boat pavilion.

The stroke of the boat, who was retiring that year, explained to her that they were not supposed to trade their precious uniforms. Now they wanted to swap for U.S. gear, a clear indication that American stock had suddenly risen in the rowing world.

In her conversation with the Germans, Claudia also learned that in addition to being twenty pounds heavier than the Americans, they were paid professionals. The stroke explained how after being selected to row, they were given jobs and paid a salary to row for their country, with monetary incentives for winning medals. As Claudia heard this, it made her silver medal feel even more valuable; it made what they had done seem even more impressive.

ONE WEEK LATER over the same Nottingham course, Harry and some of his women watched the reverse scenario occur, as the U.S. men's heavyweight team, favored to win, rowed to a disappointing fifth-place finish. The outcome was nearly the opposite of the women's results. The women's eight had beaten all but one boat; the heavyweight men had been beaten by all but one. It was a difficult day for Al Rosenberg and his former world champions, ending appropriately with rainfall.

However, even a silver medal for the men would not have meant what it did for the women that day. "We're coming up from the bottom," one of the women explained to a reporter, "and the men are coming down from the top."

A year before at the Worlds, Al Rosenberg had given his team an inspirational speech about how fortunate they were to have the opportunity to be the best in the world. No doctor or lawyer could ever make that claim, but an athlete could, however fleeting it might be. Rosenberg was an eloquent speaker who could rouse his athletes with his well-chosen words. In the same speech, he told them that nothing but a first-place finish would satisfy them, that if they won silver instead of gold, they would wake up the next morning and know that someone had rowed a better race than they had, and they would regret it. The speech had been powerful and effective. They had won the gold that year.

It was the sort of speech Parker could not, and would not, make to a team. He always trusted his crews to row as hard as they could, and never questioned their willingness to do so. Results didn't necessarily reflect effort; they could reflect many other variables, most of which, he felt, fell in his domain. When a Harvard crew lost or didn't row up to their ability, he was much more inclined to blame himself, to look back through his logbooks and see where he had failed.

In the case of this crew, there were absolutely no regrets. A silver medal for them was as good as gold, and they had honored him with their remarkable performance. They had survived the same rigors as any Parker-made crew, experienced the same high level of success. He still could not claim to have the fastest crew in the world, but the women had provided him with just the sort of rowing experience that he loved: to take an unheralded, even ignored, group of young rowers and make them into a successful team. It made the success all the more sweet and made him eager to coach them again. Rosenberg could keep the U.S. men's team; Parker wanted to continue coaching the women.

A few weeks after Nottingham, he did compose a letter expressing these thoughts, and it was one that each of the rowers would cherish for the rest of their lives, along with the roses and the silver medals:

> *To the whole "Red Rose" gang:*
>
> *I realized shortly after I left you all in the dusk at Nottingham that I owed you a much better "goodbye" than I had come up with.*
>
> *I also want to let you know how terribly proud I was of you, not only for the superb race you rowed in the final, but also for the way you raced in the heat and the repechage and handled yourselves through the whole regatta. It was a real pleasure to be associated with you.*

And . . . despite my efforts not to fully admit as much, you all must have realized that I thoroughly enjoyed working with you throughout the summer. You rowed well, and very hard, which helped, but you were also very nice people, which helped a lot more . . .

The letter went on to describe Parker's plans for them the following summer, when the women would compete in their first Olympics. Although it was yet to be decided who would coach, Parker stated that he was ready and willing to do so. There was no mention of him wanting to coach the U.S. men. He sketched out a rough timetable for next year's camp and told them he would find a way to work it around his Harvard duties. A tone of genuine excitement infused the letter, a notion that this was just the beginning for them all:

Next year. The Women's Olympic Rowing Committee meets Oct. 3rd, probably in Seattle, but possibly in the East. They will decide then how the '76 Olympic Team will be chosen: methods, dates, coaches, etc. If you have any thoughts, now is the time to let someone on the committee know of them.

I am assuming that the committee will want to continue the National Team program for the eight and am prepared to coach it if asked. And if a likely conflict with the Harvard–Yale race can be resolved.

It may mean that the camp will start in Cambridge about May 16th and that I will have to be absent from June 5th to either June 12 or June 19. Selection could begin in May, and either be concluded by June 5th or not until after June 12th or 19th. It is obviously not an ideal situation, but neither was this year's and we managed to make it work.

I hope that you all will be interested in competing for seats in the eight again and will be prepared to work just as hard to earn them. That is the only way the boat will be as fast as it was this year. If it is to be __faster__, each of you will have to find some way to row a little better, and be a little stronger and a little more fit than you were this year. If you are, and our luck prevails, maybe we can make up those two seconds, or the three or four that will be needed by July.

Have a good fall. Let me know what you are up to. And again, congratulations! You were great!

Harry

IT WAS EVERYTHING that Gail Pierson had hoped for and more. As she had predicted, all it took was the conversion of a few men like Parker and the rest of the rowing world would follow. *Sports Illustrated*, which had come to England to cover the men's racing, ended up highlighting the underdog success of the women as the only bright spot at the World Rowing Championships. Even *Time* magazine picked up the story, focusing solely on "The Red Rose Crew." Now they could go back home and finally be treated with some respect as real athletes, could return with their medals and use them as currency, a stamp of approval in the world of rowing and beyond.

After a short trip to Scotland, in fact, Gail and Sy met with a man in New York City who had plans to use their team picture for a commemorative stamp in Central America. A few months later Gail traveled to Philadelphia to attend the NAAO banquet. Together with Nancy, Anne, and Chris, she accepted a prestigious award called "The Vesper Cup," a large trophy onto which their names were later engraved. It was a great evening, filled with good will and levity. The award was presented by Emory Clark, the five seat of the U.S. Olympic gold-medal crew of 1964. Although Clark humorously described his own crew as a group of die-hard male chauvinists, he nevertheless proceeded to make note of the many similarities between them and the Red Rose group. Apparently both boats contained two rowers from Yale, a reformed sculler in the seven seat, and two people who had formerly raced in a pair. They also both had a handsome rower in the five seat.

For some of the younger rowers, who returned to their various college boathouses, the medal and the accolades that followed finally gave them greater respect among their male teammates, the men's crew coaches, and the college administrators. Carol Brown noticed a change in attitude back at Princeton and Carie Graves saw it at Wisconsin. But for Chris Ernst and Anne Warner, the medals and success didn't prove enough to initiate changes at Yale. They still didn't have access to showers after practice, and despite repeated pleas by the women's team, the permit for their small, temporary trailer had been seemingly ignored.

After Anne Warner and a few others got pneumonia from sitting in cold sweat that spring, she and Chris Ernst decided that they'd had enough. They were world-class athletes, but at Yale they were being treated like second-rate human beings.

On March 3rd, Chris and Anne made an appointment with the women's athletic director, Joni Barnett, presumably to sit down and chat one-on-one about the lack of facilities. Instead, when the two entered the small office, they brought with them a small army of nineteen women from the Yale crew team and a male reporter from the *Yale Daily News*. The women lined up in front of the athletic director's desk and soberly removed their Yale team issue sweatshirts and sweat pants. Emblazoned on their backs and chests, in blue magic marker, were the two words that said it all: *Title IX*.

Before the athletic director could react to the naked women, team captain Chris Ernst began to read a 300-word statement of purpose that had been carefully composed to go along with the "strip-in":

"These are the bodies that Yale is exploiting. On a day like today, the ice freezes on this skin. Then we sit for a half an hour as the ice melts through to meet the sweat that is soaking us from the inside . . ."

The story went out over the Associated Press wire, making the first page of the second section of *The New York Times*. It created a huge embarrassment for the prestigious university, and the shocked alumni responded quickly. Yale coach Nat Case was embarrassed by his team's bold move, but it caused a chain reaction that Anne and Chris had been waiting for, one that might have taken years if they had remained silent. The outcry from the alumni and the subsequent donations that flooded into the college were well worth the price that they paid for being privately admonished.

"Here's a thousand dollars," read one alumnus's letter, "please get Anne Warner a shower!"

One week later, a follow-up article in *The New York Times* noted that permits had been secured for the women's changing trailer, and larger plans for a permanent women's rowing facility were in the works.

THE U.S. MEN'S COACH, Al Rosenberg, had talked eloquently about the unfortunate reality that a man could never prove himself as the best doctor or lawyer in the world, but that in rowing they had the opportunity to do so. Women just wanted to be able to *be* a doctor or lawyer, or rower, or have a hot shower, if they felt like it. And for those members of the Red Rose Crew who were returning to college rowing programs, the medal and what lay behind it finally gave them validation in the eyes of male rowers, or more importantly, the self-confidence to assume their own validation as serious athletes and human beings.

To Carie Graves, this is what the rowing quest had always been about—testing her own self-imposed limits and not measuring them by the standards of those around her. A race could be won with less than full effort, and sometimes lost even when it had been rowed all out.

AFTER THE World Championships, when the eight was derigged and put away, Carie and Arthur took an overnight train to Land's

End, the westernmost tip of England. Finally they were away from rowing and the responsibilities that came with it. There, on the rugged coastline of cliffs reaching down to the sea, Arthur tried to show Carie how to surf. It was a totally frustrating experience for her. Even though she had some skill balancing a crew shell, surfing operated by the power of the waves—not by her own force. In surfing, you had to cooperate with water, to relax and react to the waves and let them move you along in the direction that they wanted to go.

It was time to head home, or at least back to Boston. There, the big decision wasn't about surfing, but about the surfer himself. Arthur and she had been getting more and more serious. But she hadn't even finished college yet, and next year were the Olympics, the real thing, the ultimate goal of her rowing career. In the end, she decided to return to Wisconsin. As much as she cared for Arthur, her mind and her heart were still in a crew shell somewhere, rowing hard, pushing herself through the pain to that special place where she felt so alive, powerful, and free. It was only through rowing that she experienced brief but wonderful moments, like the one she would describe almost a year later, training for the Montreal Olympics:

> *We were rowing on flat water and in the middle of a forty it was this exploding, all-enveloping feeling, just the most wonderful feeling I've ever had, right in the middle of a forty when I was just cranking on it for my life, just as hard as I could, and I knew right then . . .*
>
> *I remember thinking I am God. It sounds bizarre. That's what I thought. I am my own God . . . and if I died on this next stroke because I burst a blood vessel in my brain or my heart from pulling so hard, I don't care, because this is the ultimate.*

The   Red   Rose   Crew

HARRY PARKER returned to coach the U.S. women's team in 1976, assembling a crew containing several of the members of the Red Rose eight. Carie Graves, Carol Brown, and Anne Warner made the boat, which this time was stroked by Jackie Zoch. Gail Ricketson, the other spare in '75, also fought her way into the Olympic boat. Lynn Silliman returned as the cox. As Parker predicted, the competition was even harder during the Olympic year, but the U.S. eight managed a bronze behind East Germany and Russia.

Parker still coaches the Harvard varsity heavyweight crew, and at the publication of this book, will enter his fortieth season at Newell Boathouse. His crews continue to win both national and international competitions, with more frequency than any of their competitors.

CARIE GRAVES returned to Wisconsin for her senior year of college, but broke her wrist and had to sit on the sidelines as her team won the Eastern Sprints for the first time. She and teammate

Jackie Zoch would both make the 1976 Olympic eight, rowing in the six and stroke seats, respectively.

Graves would continue to row competitively for nine more years, until she finally achieved Olympic gold in Los Angeles in 1984. During her eleven-year rowing tenure, she rowed on four U.S. National Teams (1975, 1979, 1981, 1983) and three Olympic teams (1976, 1980, and 1984). The U.S. Olympic committee honored her as Female Athlete of the Year in both 1981 and 1984, and she is a two-time inductee in the National Rowing Hall of Fame. She was also the first inductee into the Women's Athletics Hall of Fame at the University of Wisconsin.

She became the Radcliffe varsity coach in 1977, the first woman hired to coach an Ivy League Crew. After winning her Olympic gold medal in Los Angeles, she retired from rowing and coaching for a while, married, and had a son named Ben. In 1989, she returned to take up the helm of the Northeastern women's crew, where she built a strong program. She is currently the head women's crew coach at the University of Texas, Austin, a new program founded as a result of Title IX legislation.

GAIL PIERSON married Sy Cromwell in 1976, after she tried out for the Olympic eight and was the last person cut from the team. She retired from serious competitive rowing when they had a daughter, Abigail. Sy developed a terminal illness and died, tragically, before she was born. Gail gave up her academic career and raised her daughter on her own. She did not, however, give up teaching and rowing altogether. At age thirteen, Abigail became her sculling protégé.

When she was sixteen, Abigail won the youth singles division in the Head of the Charles, and she continues to follow in her mother's and father's footsteps. As an undergraduate at Princeton, she was a member of the undefeated freshman crew, a part of the NCAA champion JV squad, and then a member of the lightweight varsity crew that went undefeated and won the National Championships. She is currently training with the national lightweight sculling team.

Gail was honored at the 1995 Head of the Charles for her contributions to women's rowing. Still an active sculler, she spends her time between Cambridge and New Hampshire, shuttling back and forth in her distinctive pickup truck.

LEIGH "WIKI" ROYDEN returned to Radcliffe after the World Championships, but her plans to make the 1976 Olympic eight ended when she fell from her bicycle and injured her wrist a few weeks before Parker's camp was to begin. She continued to row at Radcliffe, where she graduated cum laude in 1977 with a BS degree in physics.

She went on to get her PhD in geophysics and geology at MIT, where she currently teaches as a full professor. During her academic career, Wiki has received several prestigious awards in her field, including a Visiting Professorship Award for Women and a Faculty Award for Women Scientists, both from the National Science Foundation. Although she no longer rows, she has a bird's-eye view of the Charles River basin from her fourteenth-floor office at the MIT Department of Earth, Atmospheric and Planetary Sciences.

She has been married to Clark Burchfiel since 1983 and has two children, Benjamin and Halsey, one dog, and, at last count, six gerbils.

CLAUDIA SCHNEIDER LOCKWOOD took up sculling upon returning to California, and decided to try out for the 1976 quadrascull, coached by Tom McKibbon. After the Olympic games, she retired from rowing to pursue a career in nursing and married George Lockwood.

She currently lives in El Dorado, California, with her husband and their three children—David, Samantha, and Jonathan. They also have a couple of horses, some chickens, cats, and a dog, and lead a quiet, rural life in the foothills of the Sierras. An operating-room RN since 1979, she considers her family to be her greatest accomplishment, although her 1975 silver medal and the red rose that came with it still hang on her living room wall. The petals of the rose have now nearly all fallen.

After a twenty-year hiatus, she returned to rowing a few years ago when she teamed up with former Red Rose teammates Carol Brown, Nancy Storrs, and Carie Graves to win the Masters National Championships. The crew practiced twice before their race.

The energy and beauty of our youth diminishes and burns out. Friends come and go. Fame moves on to other recipients.

ANNE WARNER TAUBES returned to Yale, where she graduated with honors in 1977. Together with Chris Ernst, she staged the infamous Title IX "strip-in" that spring.

Anne continued her rowing career as a member of the 1976 Olympic eight, and became the first woman at Yale to earn an Olympic medal. The following year she rowed the National Team pair with Anita DeFrantz, and was both a spare sculler and a member of the 1979 National Team and the 1980 Olympic Team. After completing her degree in Russian studies at Yale, she spent a year in Bulgaria, studying indigenous folk music and dance. Upon her return to Cambridge, she founded a local women's Slavic choir, attended Harvard Law School, and married Cliff Taubes, a math professor at Harvard. Prior to having children, she worked as general counsel for Hill & Barlow, a prestigious Boston law firm.

From 1992 to 1995, Anne served as first selectman of the town of Belmont, Massachusetts, where she resides with her husband and their two children, Hannibal and Aly. She is currently vice president of business development at Leutan, a software development company.

NANCY STORRS rowed on several U.S. National Team boats, including the 1980 Olympic eight, and then back problems forced her to retire from competitive rowing. Her medals include a silver in 1978 (Worlds, New Zealand) and a gold (Worlds, Lucerne). Originally from Long Island, she now lives in Saint Catherine's, Ontario, where she is a Canadian national team coach along with her long-standing fiancé, Jack Nicholson.

In addition to crew coaching, Nancy has been a much sought-after speaker and announcer at various important regattas, including the Head of the Charles, the World Championships, and the Olympic Games. Last year, at the Worlds in St. Catherine's, just prior to announcing the results of the men's double, Nancy paged her fiancé and said the following:

"Jack, in response to that ring you gave me six years ago, the answer is *yes*."

CAROL BROWN also made Parker's 1976 Olympic eight. She was a member of several successful National Team boats, including the 1978 coxed four (silver medalists), the 1981 eight (silver), and the 1983 four. She was a member of the boycotted 1980 Olympic eight, and a spare on the 1984 gold medal eight.

After retiring from rowing in 1984, she married longtime boyfriend Lindsay Pomeroy. She has lived in Seattle since 1976, and has one little boy, Stuart, who "currently shows no evidence that rowing would be enough of an adrenaline rush for him."

Carol is currently living in France for two years, where Lindsay is working for Microsoft's European Headquarters. She completed an MBA at the University of Washington in 1998, and up until recently was very involved in both the U.S. Rowing Association and the U.S. Olympic Committee, serving several terms on the boards of directors of both organizations and serving as chair of several key USOC athlete-related program committees.

She still rows from time to time with masters programs in the

Seattle area and keeps in shape by swimming, biking, and playing tennis.

CHRIS ERNST was a spare for the 1976 Olympic pair, and shortly thereafter began to focus on sculling. At the NWRA championships in 1980, she won the heavyweight single, placed second in the heavyweight double, and was a member of the winning heavyweight quadrascull. She was the U.S. women's single sculler at the '83 Pan Am Games, and a member of the U.S. double scull in 1985. The next year, when women's lightweight events were introduced, Ernst rowed the bow seat of a U.S. women's lightweight double scull that won a gold medal on the same Nottingham course as the Red Rose Crew. Ernst and her partner, C. B. Sands, were coached by former teammate Anne Warner.

Chris was the subject of the recent documentary, "A Hero for Daisy," a biographical film that detailed her early life as a groundbreaking female athlete. She currently lives in Brookline, Massachusetts, where she runs her own business, Pipeline Plumbing.

LYNN SILLIMAN REED returned as the coxswain for the U.S. women's Olympic eight in 1976, and then took a year off to focus on her college career at Stanford. Her field of study was developmental child psychology, although she eventually went into banking and business.

She lives with her four children and two stepchildren in Point Loma, a suburb of San Diego. A born-again Christian, she is currently busy raising her one-year-old daughter, Sarah, with her husband Steven. She still enjoys running and growing roses.

DANIEL J. BOYNE is the director of Recreational Rowing at Harvard University and former varsity women's coach at Tufts University. He has published numerous articles in periodicals such as *Harvard Magazine*, *The Atlantic Monthly*, and *Wooden Boat*. He is the author of *Essential Sculling* and a former columnist for *American Rowing Magazine*. He lives in Cambridge, Massachusetts.